LEGENDS OF WARFARE

AVIATION

P-8A Poseidon

The US Navy's Newest Maritime Patrol & Antisubmarine Aircraft

JOHN GOURLEY

SCHIFFER MILITARY

4880 Lower Valley Road Atglen, PA 19310

Designed by Justin Watkinson
Type set in Impact/Minion Pro/Univers LT Std

ISBN: 978-0-7643-5922-4
Printed in China

Published by Schiffer Publishing, Ltd.
4880 Lower Valley Road
Atglen, PA 19310
Phone: (610) 593-1777; Fax: (610) 593-2002
E-mail: Info@schifferbooks.com
www.schifferbooks.com

For our complete selection of fine books on this and related subjects, please visit our website at www.schifferbooks.com. You may also write for a free catalog.

Schiffer Publishing's titles are available at special discounts for bulk purchases for sales promotions or premiums. Special editions, including personalized covers, corporate imprints, and excerpts, can be created in large quantities for special needs. For more information, contact the publisher.

We are always looking for people to write books on new and related subjects. If you have an idea for a book, please contact us at proposals@schifferbooks.com.

Acknowledgments

The author is forever indebted to those who helped in many ways to make this book become a reality. As the old saying in these sections goes, a book is never the product of a single individual. Other people, locations, events, and thoughts as well as the occasional late-night revelations all play a part. To my friends Dave Baker, Phil Blaha, Dr. Norman Friedman, Andre Jans, Dennis Jenkins, Al McQueen, and Alan Michaels, and to those I served with in the United States Air Force, I deeply appreciate your friendship and encouragement over the years, as I have moved from strictly taking photographs for my ever-expanding image archives, to writing articles and contributing pictures to other writers' projects, into writing books of my own. I especially want to thank the folks up at NAS Jacksonville, including Base Public Affairs Officer Kaylee LaRocque, Lt. j.g. Nate Shepherd, and Dominic Bellissimo of Patrol Squadron 5 "Mad Foxes," who spent time showing me around the squadron and answering questions while I checked off my "wish list" of P-8A Poseidon topics.

To my daughter, Jacqueline, who has always been a personal source of positive energy in my life experience and who also had, at times, to patiently put up with me on outings of extended photo taking and information gathering, in places as far flung as White Sands, New Mexico, to the National Museum of Naval Aviation in Pensacola, Florida. To my sister Lauren, my nephew Brandon, and my niece Marissa, each of whom has contributed to this in ways that only family members can understand and cherish.

Dedication

To all those who fly, operate, and maintain the P-8 Poseidon the world over, from bases at home to far-flung outposts half a world away. It is they who keep watch. They who ensure safe passage on the oceans while aiding those in distress, asserting the rights of all seafarers to freedom of navigation, and who will do their level best to keep the peace. If peaceful efforts fail, it is they who will engage the enemy swiftly with powerful weapons to bring aggression to a quick end.

Contents

Foreword

Several years ago, while having lunch with John Gourley, we got onto the subject of the new maritime patrol plane the US Navy was investigating to replace the venerable Lockheed P-3 Orion. This was to be a variant of the ubiquitous Boeing 737 airliner. Despite the P-3 having been derived from an airliner from a different generation, we were having a difficult time visualizing a 737 fitted with weapons under the wings and fuselage!

Nevertheless, it was obvious even then that the 737 offered a significant improvement in interior volume, power generation, and range while providing a leap ahead in technology. Using the well-understood 737 airframe and aerodynamics would minimize development risk and reduce costs, since much of the airplane could piggyback on commercial 737 production lines. It all seemed like a plausible idea. So, we ended the chat and waited.

As the years passed, the new aircraft was designated P-8 and the development process moved ahead. In 2012, John was able to shoot his first photos of the aircraft as they worked the pattern at nearby Patrick Air Force Base in Florida, doing approaches and departures from their main runway. Using the airspace at Patrick was a way to build up flight hours while avoiding the airspace congestion around their first base at Naval Air Station Jacksonville (NAS JAX). From that beginning, John opened up a file on the P-8A and kept abreast of developments as the planes became more numerous and began showing up at airshows and other events. John wanted to write about the airplane and was accumulating a wealth of photos to do so when the opportunity presented itself. When our schedules permitted, we would meet up, and some talk was always focused on the P-8A and what new photographs and information he might have on hand.

John realized that pictures alone do not make up a book, so he began digging into what makes a 737 a reality, since much of a P-8A is essentially the airliner version. Then the task of accumulating data unique to the P-8 itself was added to the material to present, in time, a great assessment of the Poseidon and its capabilities. The final phase was a visit to NAS JAX, during which the folks of the Public Affairs Office and of VP-5, the "Mad Foxes," scheduled a tour of their facilities. With all of this accomplished, John has managed to create a book that is detailed in all aspects. Since this may well be the first substantial book published on the P-8A, John has undertaken a great effort to showcase the plane from many angles, from the aircrews, maintainers, and the work they do, to the flying and missions they accomplish. Exterior and interior features are captioned in detail. The book should have great appeal to modelers, aviation enthusiasts, researchers, and historians. It will certainly become a valued and necessary reference for the foreseeable future. This has been John's goal from the outset, and I have always appreciated his updates as the book came together. I hope that everyone else who has an interest in naval aviation will agree.

Dennis R. Jenkins, author
Cape Canaveral, Florida
December 2018

Introduction

The P-8A Poseidon is replacing the trusted and reliable P-3 Orion in the roles of antisubmarine warfare, ocean surveillance, and naval intelligence gathering. Based on the Boeing commercial 737 series of airliner, the P-8A combines twin turbofan-engine economy with the latest in technologies for detecting, analyzing, and investigating targets on the surface, underwater, and in the shallow littoral regions. Threats can be engaged with weapons such as air-launched antiship missiles, and torpedoes designed to hunt down and destroy subsurface craft.

The P-8A is also capable of search-and-rescue (SAR) missions, with radar capable of several modes of operation to find objects from small boats to life rafts. Observers seated on both sides of the cabin can visually scan the sea surface through large side windows and quickly report any visual sightings. Equipment capable of use by victims of a maritime accident can also be carried and dropped to enable repairs or aid in recovery by supporting search vessels or helicopters.

The P-8A Poseidon is packed with the latest hardware for its intended roles and can also transmit data in real time to other platforms as varied as aircraft, unmanned aerial vehicles (UAVs), surface ships, satellites, and ground stations. A multipurpose sensor turret can observe, target, and record images in daylight or in darkness. An electronic-support-measures array of antennas picks up signals, analyzes them, and displays to the aircrew in seconds the electronic order of battle, or shows vital intelligence information obtained during surveillance flights used for future planning and tactical operations. Sonobuoy launchers can be loaded before a flight begins and can dispense buoys quickly so they can transmit data on undersea activity. Smoke flares or underwater sensors can also be dropped either to mark targets, as in the former case, or to record subsurface marine dynamic conditions, as in the latter case.

The P-8A is also equipped for self-defense, with a large aircraft infrared countermeasures system that has the ability to detect in several bandwidths the approach of a hostile missile. This system acts automatically to feed data to a device that aims an intense, pulsed, coded beam of invisible energy at the missile target seeker. This results in the missile flying harmlessly past the aircraft or detonating prematurely, as the P-8A continues on its mission to provide a persistent, continuous presence above the world's oceans.

The P-8A is already making its impact felt in reduced maintenance man-hours, reduced transit times to patrol sectors, greater range and endurance, improved aircrew comfort, and increased coordination resulting from a revamped, user-friendly cabin arrangement while completing demanding mission objectives. Other nations are already buying the P-8 or are showing interest in acquiring this platform, since in many cases nations still using the P-3 are wanting to upgrade to a new aircraft. The P-8A has now proven itself to be a vital node in the overall concepts of net-centric warfare and enhanced command-control and communications (C3) capabilities in naval operations.

The name "Poseidon" refers to the mythical Greek god of the sea. He was also known as having dominion over earthquakes and storms and could unleash his fury with little provocation when agitated. His three-pronged trident was the symbol of that power. Today's Poseidon keeps watch over the seven seas, to maintain and preserve sea lines of communication and free trade. If challenged or compelled to act, the modern Poseidon can use a form of the symbolic trident in the shapes of torpedoes, mines, and air-launched missiles, to assert the rights of nations to navigate the oceans safely, unimpeded, and without hindrance, protecting sailors, passengers, and traders everywhere.

CHAPTER 1
P-8A Background

The United States Navy, in the mid-1980s, initiated a plan to replace a portion of the P-3 Orion fleet, since some of this type would be at the end of their service lives by the 1990s. P-3s had been introduced into regular use in the early 1960s, with many having been kept operational through various upgrades, depot maintenance, and modification programs. In January 1987, a competition was begun by the Navy to develop a P-3 replacement. This request for proposals (RFP) had three responses from industry: Boeing offered up a modified 757 airliner as a possible P-3 replacement, McDonnell Douglas brought a modified MD-90 airliner variant into the RFP phase, and Lockheed proposed a modernized P-3, with updated avionics and new engines/propellers. Because cost of the replacement program was of paramount concern, the Navy decided in the end to purchase an overhauled P-3 design in October 1988. This submission also appeared to be the cheapest of the three put forth for consideration. This P-3 Orion variant, provisionally labeled "P-3G," would be a production run of around 125 new-build airframes. A timeline for construction of all examples would run from 1997 to 2001.

Total program costs were estimated to be in the range of $600 million to $750 million, with a unit cost of around $57 million each. In January 1989, the Defense Acquisition Board (DAB) recommended that a full-scale development (FSD) phase be started. The aircraft designation was revised to P-7A and was later labeled as the LRAACA, or long-range air ASW-capable aircraft. The aircraft, had it been built, would have looked very much like the P-3C Orion still in use today. The fuselage would have had an 8-foot extension, and the tail fin height would have been lower. It was slated to have a complement of thirteen or more aircrew members. Four General Electric T407-GE-400 turboprops of 6,000 horsepower each would have spun five-bladed, advanced-design composite propellers and would have had a range of 2,470 miles (2,146 nautical miles or 3,975 kilometers [km]). Maximum

speed would have been 410 miles per hour (660 km per hour). Empty weight would have been 105,000 pounds (47,627 kilograms [kg]), and gross weight was projected at 165,000 pounds (74,843 kg). Maximum takeoff weight would have been 171,350 pounds (77,723 kg). An internal bomb bay, as on the P-3, would have had the capacity for carrying up to 1,545 pounds (3,400 kg) of ordnance. Up to twelve underwing pylons would carry mines, torpedoes, antiship missiles, or bombs.

The P-7A interior would be outfitted with glass displays as well as a head-up display (HUD) for the flight crew, and the P-3C Update IV suite of ASW gear would have gone into the cabin. Sonobuoy capacity was to be 112 loaded before flight, with an additional thirty-eight ready for reloading while in flight. The wing pylons could also be hung with canisters holding up to 150 more. Also planned for inclusion were infrared suppression of engine exhaust heat, infrared countermeasures (IRCM) hardware, the magnetic anomaly detector or aft-protruding (MAD) tail "sting" (a prominent feature peculiar to all ASW P-3s), radar-warning receivers (RWRs), and an electro-optical turret sensor for viewing objects in the normal/infrared wavelengths.

The P-7A program incurred, in November 1989, a cost overrun of $300 million due to schedule conflicts and more time needed to adapt to new design assembly procedures. In July 1990, the Navy declared Lockheed in default of the contract and stopped the P-7A program due to lengthy delays and projected rises in life-cycle project costs. Other proposals, such as the Orion 2000 RMPA (replacement maritime patrol aircraft) for the British Royal Navy and P-3 Valkyrie, all similar to the P-7 design, failed to generate any orders or be put into production.

No discussion of the P-3 Orion is justified without illustrations to accompany this historical account. The images provide a glimpse into many P-3 versions and interior configurations.

A P-3C of Patrol Squadron VP-30, buzz number LL-44, in the TPS (tactical paint scheme) used to blend in more effectively in clouds and sea surfaces. *Author*

An EP-3A extended-area test system (EATS) is outfitted for reception of signals from intercontinental ballistic missile (ICBM) testing. Has no MAD or ASW gear. *Author*

A P-3 AEW+C, BuNo 154575 / N148CS, is modified with a rotodome also used by the E-2C Hawkeye, used by the US Customs and Border Patrol as an airborne surveillance platform. *Author*

This RP-3D, BuNo 153443, was modified for use in PROJECT SEASCAN to gather data on ocean characteristics. Operating squadron was VXN-8. *Author*

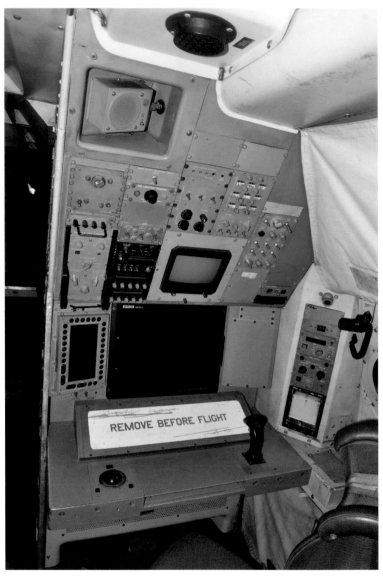

P-3C, BuNo 158933, TACCO station 3 arrangement in January 1993. The round cathode ray tube (CRT) screen dominates the console. To right is MAD panels and readout. Joystick controls the AAS-36 infrared detection system (IRDS) turret. *Author*

Another TACCO station 3 on P-3C, BuNo 158225, in 2017. Trackball, joystick relocated, with panels replaced as upgrades became available. Liquid crystal display (LCD) screen gave a major improvement in visual interaction with mission graphics. *Author*

A Canadian CP-140A Arcturus, one of many export versions of the P-3. Three of this variant are used for Arctic patrol flights and have no ASW equipment installed. *Author*

A P-3A Aerostar, former BuNo 151361, has been adapted for use as a water bomber. Red and black make the plane easier to see when in use. *Author*

P-3C with the APS-149 LSRS or littoral surveillance radar system. Aircraft is at Kadena AB in Okinawa. A similar radar, the APS-154, is used by the P-8A. *Jeffery Schultze / USAF*

Yet another variant is this WP-3D, used for weather research and for penetrating hurricanes to measure their intensity and growth potential. Ex-, BuNo 159875 / N43RF used by NOAA. *Author*

P-3C antisubmarine warfare improvement program (AIP) 158919 in October 2004. A pilot color high-resolution display (PCHRD) viewing screen has replaced the older round unit with a lighter and more capable one. The AIP enhancement included a new mission computer, and GPS replaced the OMEGA navigation system. JTIDS (joint tactical information distribution system) was also added to connect the P-3 to a comprehensive data-link network. Such upgrades kept the P-3 fleet relevant over the lifetime of exceptional Navy service. The complicated-looking vertical instrument panel is actually quite organized. Flight-essential gauges are within the pilot line of sight. The engine instruments are clustered together, *at center*. Above them are four T-handles for activating the fire suppression system. The gray wheel (*at far left*) is the tiller, used for nosewheel steering while taxiing. *Author*

CHAPTER 2
Birth of the P-8A

With the P-7A unfunded and not built, the Navy began, in 1997, a two-year study into the acquisition of a mission maritime aircraft (MMA). Time was of the essence, since the P-3 fleet still had no replacement on the horizon, and the retirement of the ES-3A Shadow carrier based electronic intelligence (ELINT) platform (a variant of the S-3 Viking ASW aircraft) further strained the EP-3 Orion types, since they had to take on ever more mission hours to fill the gap left not only by the ES-3As, but by the reduction in numbers of S-3B Vikings outfitted for ASW taskings. Eventually, a replacement for the EP-3E ARIES II–series ELINT planes was also included in this MMA specification.

In 2000, a mission statement was agreed upon, stating that the new plane had to fulfill roles in antisubmarine warfare (ASW), antisurface warfare (ASuW), and signal intelligence collection (SIGINT), as well as to carry/launch weapons and be able to assist in search-and-rescue (SAR) flights. New missions such as littoral operations and antipiracy and counterterrorism roles were included. The Navy also initiated an analysis of alternatives for extending the lifetimes of the P-3s in service until the new plane was ready. These included overhauling airframes with new wings, engines, and cockpit instrument panels. Other options explored adapting a current airframe type for MMA use, or starting from scratch with a clean-sheet design.

In 2002, Raytheon was awarded a $223,000 contract from Naval Air Systems Command to look at P-3/EP-3 production, including enhancements to the airframes, flight decks, and engines in order to enhance payload capacity and boost time on station. Lockheed Martin checked into the same upgrades plus new wings under a $493,000 contract. Boeing was also provided funds for a concept-exploration look at modifying the 737-800 airliner for MMA missions. Northrop Grumman received a contract for $500,000 to propose a network of unmanned aerial vehicles linked to a diminished number of manned platforms.

With all these alternative options completed by June 2004, the Navy chose the Boeing adaptation of the 737-800 airliner as the winner of the MMA successor to the P-3 Orion. Boeing was then awarded a contract totaling $3.89 billion for the next phase,

known as the system development and demonstration (SDD) contract. Thus began the integration of hardware and research to provide the software, mission, and simulation training systems. A team of companies was created, with each providing components assembled by Boeing:

CFM International: provides the CFM56-7B engines

Northrop Grumman: provides the directional infrared countermeasures (DIRCM) system, data links, and mission-planning hardware

Raytheon: provides the APY-10 and APS 154 radars and Mk. 54 torpedo

GE Aviation: supplies the flight management system (FMS) and stores management system

Spirit Aerosystems: builds and ships the fuselage and tail sections

BAE Systems: produces the mission computing and display systems and flight deck panels

Included in the SDD contract were five test airframes: S1 for static testing, S2 for fatigue test work, T1, T2, and T3. Three more examples, T4, T5, and T6, were also included for test flight work.

A systems requirements review (SRR) was conducted in September 2004, noting several minor changes. Wind tunnel testing at low and high airspeeds was conducted from October to December 2004. The year 2005 saw a successful integrated baseline review, system functional review, and preliminary design review. The P-8A designation was assigned on March 22. Ground tests began in the third quarter. In February 2006, wind tunnel work involved weapons separation tests.

T1 test airframe, BuNo 167951 / N541BA, on an evaluation flight. The N-number is a temporary registration while the aircraft undergoes builder's flight trials. *Boeing Corp. photo*

P-8A of VX-20 flies over the Chesapeake and DDG-1000 *Zumwalt* in October 2016. Both platforms can share information on targets, intelligence, and images and video. *Erik Hildebrandt / US Navy*

P-8A with a P-3C over NAS Patuxent River in Maryland. The arrival of the Poseidon began a new era in ASW, ASuW, intelligence, and surveillance capabilities. *Liz Goettee / US Navy*

The nineteenth P-8A built, BuNo 168759, lifts off on a delivery flight to join VP-16, the "War Eagles," from Seattle to NAS JAX in November 2014. *US Navy*

On January 9, 2007, Poseidon was announced as the aircraft name. In July, a critical design review was conducted and passed, and in December, Spirit Aerosystems started production of the T1 test aircraft fuselage, which was delivered to Boeing in March 2008. The wings were attached in May, and in July the S1 static test airframe was completed and production began on the second P-8A. T1, with Bureau Number (BuNo) 167951 / N541BA, made its first flight on April 25, 2009. In 2010, T1 was flown to NAS Patuxent River, Maryland, for more airworthiness testing, including weapon carriage and release trials. One of the test planes dropped six sonobuoys in three low passes in October. Low-rate initial-production lot 1 (LRIP-1) of ten aircraft was started. In January 2011, the full range of static tests was completed. In July, the first P-8A, BuNo 168428, was flown and eventually delivered to Navy squadron VP-30 in March 2012. The second example, T2, BuNo 167953 / N44BA, first flew on June 5, 2009, and was tasked with mission systems integration and checkout, with time spent in the McKinley Climatic Laboratory, at Eglin AFB in Florida, for tests in extreme-weather conditions. The third flying example, T3, BuNo 167954 / N397DS, took its maiden flight on September 23, 2009, and was used for performance and electromagnetic testing.

In January 2013, the last LRIP-1 examples were delivered. The LRIP-2 lot of twelve was delivered in December 2013; LRIP-3 numbers fourteen examples. The estimated unit cost of $126 million (in fiscal year [FY] 2004 dollars) is calculated on a production run for the US Navy of 108 aircraft. In the first three years of production, thirty-six aircraft are expected to be delivered. Total program cost was estimated in FY 2013 to amount to $33.638 billion, and in FY 2015, unit cost had increased to $256.5 million. In June, a P-8A flew with the APS-154 advanced airborne sensor (AAS), a long, canoe-type pod containing an active electronically scanned array (AESA) radar.

The P-8A is designed with space for additional growth over its fleet service lifetime. A major subvariant, from nineteen to twenty-six examples (possibly to be designated EP-8B), with operator stations for fourteen aircrew and a sealed weapons bay replaced with antennas, would eventually replace the EP-3E ARIES II type. The EP-3E version serves as a dedicated ELINT/SIGINT platform, with many modifications and fairings not common to mainstream P-3 types. Other P-8 modifications, such as the temporary fitting of the APS-154 radar pod as well as upgrades to ESM, self-defense suites, and weapon-carrying capabilities, all are likely as the type is integrated fully into Navy plans and operations.

Operational units increase as planes are delivered. At present, seven frontline squadrons of six planes each reside at NAS Jacksonville; twelve planes are used for training. NAS Whidbey Island, Washington, has three frontline squadrons, and Hawaii will eventually host three squadrons. Upgrades to the P-8A include the Spiral 1 program, which includes P-3C updates already in effect being transferred to P-8A hardware. A Spiral II upgrade will begin in 2017. Some P-3s will also get enhancements in order to keep them effective until they are retired.

Foreign Sales

India has bought eight P-8I Neptune planes for $2.1 billion. Deliveries were made from 2012 to 2015. They have an aft-facing radar, a magnetic-anomaly detector, and the ability to carry/drop weapons such as depth charges.

Australia ordered eight aircraft, with options for four more, replacing RAAF P-3Cs.

The **Republic of Korea** intends to buy six P-8As through a foreign military sales (FMS) arrangement, ultimately replacing P-3Cs.

The **United Kingdom** intends to buy nine Poseidon MRA1 airframes plus supporting hardware for $3.87 billion to fill an open, land-based maritime patrol requirement when all Nimrod-type ASW planes are retired.

Norway is likely to order five in the 2022–23 time frame to replace P-3Ns.

New Zealand will purchase four to replace P-3Ks beginning in 2023 for $1.46 billion.

Saudi Arabia intends to order examples to patrol the Arabian Gulf and Red Sea.

Tour of a P-8A by Deputy Defense Secretary Bob Work in April 2016, on the assembly line at the Boeing Corporation facility at Renton, Washington. Visible are many items already installed along the inner fuselage, such as insulation, air ducts, wires, and hydraulic lines. Several hanging wire harnesses are intended to eventually be attached to operator consoles, intercom systems, computers, and communications networks. *Clydell Kinchen / US Army*

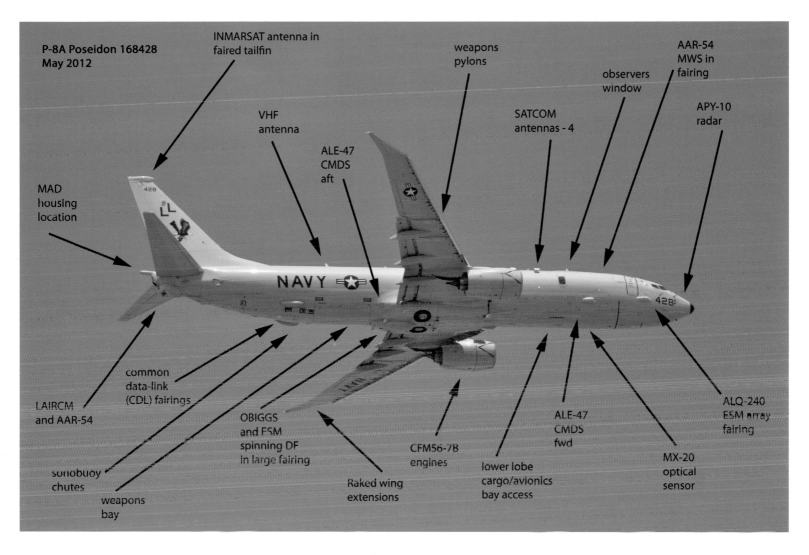

P-8A Poseidon 168428
May 2012

INMARSAT antenna in
faired tailfin

weapons
pylons

AAR-54
MWS in
fairing

observers
window

VHF
antenna

SATCOM
antennas - 4

APY-10
radar

ALE-47
CMDS
aft

MAD
housing
location

LAIRCM
and AAR-54

common
data-link
(CDL) fairings

OBIGGS
and FSM
spinning DF
in large fairing

ALE-47
CMDS
fwd

ALQ-240
ESM array
fairing

sonobuoy
chutes

CFM56-7B
engines

MX-20
optical
sensor

weapons
bay

Raked wing
extensions

lower lobe
cargo/avionics
bay access

P-8A Poseidon, BuNo 168428, VP-30 LL-428, in May 2012. *Photo taken by / items of interest labeled by author*

P-8A twentieth production example, BuNo168760, heads for squadron assignment at NAS JAX. The gray paint scheme has been found to be most effective in most flight situations with clouds / dark skies. *US Navy / Boeing photo*

Australian, Indian, and US P-8As together at Pearl Harbor as RIMPAC 2018 gets underway. The exercise involved twenty-five nations, forty-six ships, five submarines, and 200 planes. *Kevin A. Flinn / US Navy*

P-8A, BuNo 169009, flies by Mount Baker during a training drill in May 2017. VP-4 uses the tail code YD to identify the "Skinny Dragons," who are based at NAS Whidbey Island. *Juan S. Sua / US Navy*

Royal Australian Air Force P-8A, BuNo A47-007, the seventh example of the RAAF variant, at Hickam AFB, Hawaii, in May 2018. Export P-8s are outfitted to customer needs. *Heather Redman / USAF*

This P-8 fuselage never took to the air. Instead, the S1 example shown here at the Naval Airworthiness Center Weapons Survivability Laboratory at China Lake was used for tests in live-fire events to determine ability to withstand ballistic damage. It also was used to design an effective fire suppression system in July 2012. *Dan Kunkel / US Navy*

CHAPTER 3
Design and Specifications

Fuselage/wings: Fuselage derived from the Boeing 737-800 series of airliner. Wings are used from the Boeing 737-900 series. Constructed of aluminum, titanium, and composites. P-8A is similar in configuration and outfit to the military C-40 Clipper and 737 AEW+C types.

Dimensions: Length: 129.5 feet (39.47 meters), wingspan: 123.6 feet (37.64 meters), height: 42.1 feet (12.83 meters)

Range: Exceeds 1,381 miles (1,200 nautical miles, 2,222 km), with on-station time of four hours

Operational ceiling: 500 feet (200 feet above the sea surface lowest limit) up to 41,000 feet

Crew complement: In most flight scenarios, a crew of nine: three flight crew, five mission operators, one in-flight technician

Maximum takeoff weight (MTOW): 189,200 pounds (85,820 kg)

Wingtips: Changed from winglets to backswept tips, increasing overall performance and reducing susceptibility to icing. Electrically deiced.

Radome: Composite structure contains surveillance antennas and the APY-10 multimode radar, a modification of the APS-137D. Six conductive diverter strips decrease the electrical-charge energy from a radome lightning strike, directing the current aft into the airframe to be dissipated.

Cockpit windows: Same as on commercial 737s, except overhead brow windows deleted. Side windows can be opened inward and slid aft. In an emergency, the pilot and copilot can exit the aircraft if necessary, by means of escape ropes. Weight capacity of each rope is 300 pounds.

Aerial refueling: Via UARRSI (universal aerial refueling slipway installation) on top of the fuselage aft of cockpit section. Fills center fuel tank when used. Compatible with KC-135, KC-10, and KC-46 flying-boom fueling methods only.

SATCOM: Satellite communication antennas are four white, batwing-shaped units along both upper sides of the forward fuselage. Can connect to the MILSTAR, MUOS, and other satellites to transmit real-time data and video and also receive data, including by use of the JTIDS Link-16 system.

Global Positioning System (GPS): The GPS antijam system 1 hardware (GAS-1) is used. Located atop the forward fuselage.

Emergency locator transmitter (ELT): The ELT operates on 121.5/243.0 and 406.0 radio frequencies.

ESM: The ALQ-240 electronic support system consists of fixed arrays along fuselage sides and in a spinning DF (direction finder) unit in a large belly radome just aft of the main gear wheel bays. Totally automatic.

OBIGGS: Onboard inert gas–generating system. Also contained within large belly radome, used to inject a nitrogen-enriched air (NEA) compound into the center, auxiliary, and wing fuel tanks, thereby lowering combustible fuel vapor levels to safe limits.

ALE-47: Countermeasures dispensers. Located in modules along the forward fuselage, along both sides, and aft of the wing-root fairing (both sides), for a total of four, to give 360 degrees of coverage. Can eject flares to defeat infra-red guided missiles or chaff cartridges to lure away radar-guided weapons.

MX-20 optical sensor (formerly designated MX-20HD): Located in the forward belly. Stored internally to be lowered for use. The device gives optical-imaging capabilities in normal and infrared wavelengths. Solid-state internal components capable of five-axis stabilization.

Deicing: EMDS (electromechanical expulsion deicing system) used on wingtips and empennage. Wings use a WTAI (wing thermal anti-icing system) to blow hot air onto the three inboard leading-edge slats. Electric deicing warms the windshield transparencies.

Wing movable surfaces: Four flaps, eight slats. Four spoilers reduce lift and increase drag; also used for roll control. Krueger flaps under wing leading edges.

Batteries: Two 24-volt NiCad (nickel-cadmium) types. Accessed in chin compartment aft of radome.

Engines: Two CFM56-7B types, dual-rotor axial flow turbofans of approximately 27,300 pounds of static thrust (ST) each

Integrated drive generators (IDGs): One on each engine, providing three-phase 115 volt (400 Hz) alternating-current (AC) power

IFF (identification friend or foe): UPX-43, which also provides automatic dependent surveillance–broadcast (ADS-B) capability

Advanced airborne sensor (AAS): AAS is designated the APS-154. Replaces the APS-149 used by the P-3C. Used for intelligence, surveillance, reconnaissance, and targeting (ISR&T) missions.

Landing gear: Tricycle-type, air/oil shock struts. Main gears have disc-type carbon-fiber brakes. Antiskid and autobraking included.

Missile-warning system (MWS): AAR-54 initially. Aircraft delivered later have UV/IR (ultraviolet/infrared) sensors. Located on forward fuselage, on the aft lower-tail-cone fairing, and on belly. These cue the AAQ-24 DIRCM (directional infrared countermeasures) turret on where to aim an energy beam at an incoming missile.

LAIRCM: Large aircraft infrared countermeasures. When signaled by AAR-54 or UV/IR sensor array, the turret, located under the tail-cone aft fairing, aims and emits a beam of intense, pulsed, coded energy at the seeker head of an incoming missile.

Common data link (CDL): The CDL fairings contain steerable dish antennas that transmit/receive streams of information to friendly platforms such as ships, planes, UAVs, or ground stations. Operates in Ku band, at 274 megabits per second. Belly has a single CDL omni antenna.

Fuel capacity: 10,856 US gallons, distributed among five internal tank groups (main tank 1; main tank 2; center, forward, and aft tank groups).

Weapon pylon stations: Eleven total. Four wing locations of bomb release units or BRU-76; 1,491 pounds of capacity to carry AGM-84 Harpoon or AGM-84K SLAM-ER (standoff land attack missile–extended response) and associated AWW-13 data link pod. Two fuselage stations and five in the weapons bay, all of the BRU-75 type, capable of 650 pounds of capacity. All are of the pneumatic-release design, eliminating pyrotechnic, cartridge-actuated, device-related issues.

INMARSAT: The international maritime satellite system, using an AMT-50A high-gain antenna (HGA) unit. Installed at the very top of the tail fin, inside a composite fairing. Antenna locks onto and maintains signal integrity as aircraft flies or maneuvers.

Weapons bay: Located aft of the main gear wells and OBIGGS/ESM radome, up to five BRU-75s can carry Mk. 54 lightweight torpedoes, Mk. 62 Quickstrike mines, or UNI PAC II air-drop survival kits. Two sets of hinged bay doors are hydraulically operated.

Sonobuoy chutes: Several located aft of weapons bay. Three chutes connected to pressurized ten-round rotary carousels in the aft crew cabin. Used to drop A-sized types (5-inch diameter) of the GPS-enabled, VHF-band-transmitting SSQ-53G passive, SSQ-62F active, SSQ-101 multistatic noncoherent-source, and SSQ-125 multistatic coherent source types. Single-sonobuoy launchers (SSL, 3-inch-diameter types) can manually deploy the SSQ-36 bathythermograph, to determine seawater temperature profiles, and the Mk. 39 expendable mobile ASW training target (EMATT). Also released are Mk. 58 marine location markers (smoke flares) and sound underwater signal (SUS) devices, and they can also be used for emergency jettison of internal stores. Sonobuoy capacity, if fully loaded before flight with cabin racks full, is ninety-six (forty-eight in each rack). If three rotary launchers are installed and full, containing ten buoys each, capacity total is 126.

Auxiliary power unit (APU): A model 131-9B located in tail cone, aft of lower ESM/DIRCM fairing. Provides 90 kVA to 32,000 feet / 66 kVA to 41,000 feet. On the ground, the APU provides 90 kVA AC power for ECS (environmental control system—air conditioning); compressed air used for main engine starting.

Interior configuration: At the very forward end of the crew cabin, cockpit instrument panel is of all-glass displays, with flight management system and a head-up display for the pilot. A tiller wheel for the pilot provides nosewheel steering when on the airfield. Aft of flight deck are racks for radar avionics, crew lavatory/galley, and two aircrew rest seats facing forward. Normal crew entry door can be accessed by an internally stowed airstair. Power distribution racks and two observer stations with swiveling seats are farther aft. Six crew-ditching-station aft-facing seats are across from the five operator stations, lined up along the right cabin wall. Room for a sixth station is projected for future growth options,

to be located aft of the left overwing emergency exit. A mission enclosure, communications/mission racks, and a crew mission-planning area of four seats with table along the right wall are in this section. Aft of this are dual racks for sonobuoy storage and up to three (two along right wall, one along left wall) pressurized rotary carousel launchers. The floor aft of this has three single sonobuoy launchers installed (one to right, two to left). Another mission equipment enclosure attached to the left wall, with the free-fall chute next to it, is by the access door in the left aft maintenance cabin. Aft of this is the pressure cabin aft dome. There are emergency air-breathing (EAB) devices and six portable fire extinguishers placed at strategic/easy-access locations. Interior emergency exit-lighting floor strips operate for ten minutes after a total power failure to guide crew members in dark/smoke-filled conditions to exit hatches. Two overwing exit hatches are hinged to raise hatch up and clear of the exit space onto the upper wing-root section surfaces for egress.

P-8A of VP-5 "Mad Foxes" poses at Atsugi Airbase in Japan during 2014, with a Kawasaki P-1. Both aircraft fulfill similar roles, and as a type are known generally as LRMPA (long-range maritime patrol aircraft). *Douglas Wojciechowski / US Navy*

P-8A ACTIVE SQUADRONS

Squadron	Tail code	Station
VP-4 "Skinny Dragons"	YD	NAS Whidbey Island, WA
VP-5 "Mad Foxes"	LA	NAS Jacksonville, FL
VP-8 "Tigers"	LC	NAS Jacksonville
VP-9 "Golden Eagles"	PD	NAS Whidbey Island
VP-10 "Red Lancers"	LD	NAS Jacksonville
VP-16 "War Eagles"	LF	NAS Jacksonville
VP-26 "Tridents"	LK	NAS Jacksonville
VP-30 "Pro's Nest"	LL	NAS Jacksonville
VP-45 "Pelicans"	LN	NAS Jacksonville
VP-47 "Golden Swordsmen"	RD	NAS Whidbey Island
VX-1 "Pioneers"	JA	NAS Patuxent River, MD

P-8A, BuNo 168430, of VP-16 "War Eagles" LF-430 at NAS Point Mugu, California, on temporary assignment for predeployment training in April 2015. *US Navy*

Notes on Markings

The P-8A aircraft follow standard formats for markings, as do all US military–operated aircraft of every type.

The **Bureau Number** or BuNo (also widely known as a "tail number") is assigned by the military to an aircraft once it has been built, and meets the requirements for service acceptance. This number is, in the Navy case, a six-digit line of numbers, issued one at a time or in blocks. Exceptions occur if BuNos are canceled for planes not built, lost, or transferred/sold to other nations, which usually adopt their own identification system. In US Air Force BuNo listings, the first two digits indicate the fiscal year the aircraft was accepted for government use.

The **Manufacturer's Serial Number** (MSN) is a documentation annotation (usually five digits) assigned by the airplane builder during construction. This usually refers to a particular airframe during factory assembly and postdelivery warranty / depot maintenance purposes. The MSN is usually not prominently displayed on aircraft once delivered. In rare cases, the MSN has been used as a tail number.

The **Modex Number** indicates, in the case of the P-8A, a squadron two-letter code, followed by three numbers. These codes can be assigned as a series such as the letters LF, LY, LR, or LM, along with numbers in a given series such as 400 (or 4XX) codes (e.g., -401, -458, -466) that a squadron has chosen, or as in the P-8A case, by using the last three digits of the BuNo. Modex numbers are also commonly called **Buzz Numbers**, referring to their original use. To identify aircraft violating altitude regulations, by flying low or "buzzing" over populated regions, the military devised this marking scheme to allow observers to positively identify the offending aircraft.

On the P-8A, the nose three-digit code is 20 inches in height. The word "NAVY," on the aft fuselage, is 36 inches high. The color star and bars, or **Roundel**, is 48 inches in height. The dark-blue paint used is federal standard (FS)15044, while the red stripe uses FS 11136. The white star and bars are done in FS 17925. The P-8A fuselage, wings, and engine nacelles/pylons are painted in BAC (Boeing Aircraft Corporation) 707 Gloss Grey.

P-8A, BuNo 168434, with type aircraft above. NAVAIR is the command, with emblem, that developed and produced the P-8A design. Black paint is federal standard (FS) shade 17038. P-8A is 2 inches high. BuNo is 4 inches high. *Author*

The same aircraft, showing 434 on nose. This is the last three numbers, along with LN, denoting the Modex or Buzz Number. The number "434" is in smaller digits on top of the tail fin. The pelican artwork is the squadron symbol of VP-45; Modex is LN-434. *Author*

P-8A, BuNo 167951, of test and evaluation squadron VX-20 flies over the Chesapeake Bay region during test flight number 159, which checked flight-handling qualities and stall margins, in January 2012. This view with low-angle sun highlights features such as the spine antennas, satcom batwing aerials, and the three starboard (right side) cabin egress points. *Greg L. Davis / US Navy*

P-8A, BuNo 167954, drops the first inert Mk. 54 torpedo during weapon bay testing over the Atlantic Test Range in October 2011. An add-on kit to the torpedo with wings will allow for drops at heights up to 30,000 feet. Line with drogue chute attached to tail is equipment used during flight testing. Photo-calibration markings have been placed in the weapons-bay area and doors for postflight accurate drop dynamics analysis. *US Navy*

In another flight test, P-8A, BuNo 167954, assigned to VX-20, has inert air-training missile (ATM-84) Harpoon antiship missiles underwing. To record the airdrop event, cameras are attached inboard of the wingtip, on the belly and aft ventral areas. The missile bodies, pylons, and flap track fairing are adorned with photo-calibration markings. Tests such as these are essential to ensure that the weapons can be cleared for carriage and clean separation when in fleet use. *US Navy*

P-8A, BuNo 167951, the former T1 prototype flight example, releases ATM-84 Harpoon missile shapes in an actual test of weapon separation from the underwing pylons. This air-launched variant has a range of 120 nautical miles, weighs 1,145 pounds, and has 100 pounds of fuel and a high-explosive semi-armor-piercing warhead of 488.5 pounds. *Erik Hildebrandt / US Navy*

P-8A, BuNo 167953, former T3 prototype flying example, is viewed inside the integrated battlespace simulation and test (IBST) anechoic chamber. This testing phase is conducted to ensure that all the electronic systems on board operate without interference from other components that radiate radio frequency (RF) energy. Energy-absorbing cones line the floors, walls, and ceilings in this time-exposure view. *Naval Air Warfare Center photo*

P-8A Ground Simulators: Cabin Views

Before any aircrews are qualified to fly, operate systems, or deploy as part of a squadron, they must prove proficiency by spending time in simulators. These exist as cockpit flight decks, and cabin mission operator station mockups. In these settings, mission evaluator instructors are part of the action. They can set up scenarios as the pilots "fly" the plane and specialists operate their consoles as they are presented with situations ranging from a search-and-rescue (SAR) call to a hit on the ESM array indicating the presence of a hostile-vessel search radar. The sensor turret operator might be scanning the sea and find a life raft or even stumble upon the periscope of a submerged submarine. How the crews react and the procedures they use all are observed, and the steps they take are monitored. The action can be stopped to give advice as the operation unfolds. The mission can proceed from that moment or be set back to an earlier time for more-effective measures to be employed once a scene is repeated.

In the cockpit, a smooth, uneventful flight scene over the ocean can suddenly be interrupted with dark skies, rain, and lightning, with some turbulence mixed in. Other issues may range from an outright engine failure to a loss of cabin air pressurization. Tactical inputs might involve a missile attack, establishing a search pattern, or setting up a flight profile to launch a torpedo.

In the cabin, inputs can vary, from deploying sonobuoys in an effective line during a submarine hunt to planning out an attack on a hostile guided-missile destroyer closing in on an aircraft carrier surface action group. Radio traffic, sharing data among other platforms, or messages received and acted on all can be saved and replayed to improve and refine tactics. The same mission can be run again, coming to a successful conclusion, or else might have a few extra unknowns thrown in, such as the failure of an onboard system that the crew must work around to achieve a favorable outcome. It has been proven many times that simulators are so realistic that students feel as though it were a real-world undertaking.

An RAF aircrew of Squadron Leaders Andy Bull and Mark Faulds flies an ASW mission as Lt. Brett Eckert of VP-30 watches. He can interact and add inputs on his computer, which has programmed this simulated flight. *David Giorda / US Navy*

The Patuxent River Systems Integrated Laboratory (PAXSIL) training device allows a P-8 crew to work together to train while developing tactics and test aircraft configuration. *US Navy*

Lt. j.g. Ataturk (*left*) and Lt. j.g. Nicholas Horton of VP-16 fly a P-8A during the search for Malaysian Airlines flight 370 while deployed with the Navy's 7th Fleet. *Eric A. Pastor / US Navy*

The cockpit scene of a VP-5 "Mad Foxes" P-8A as the throttles, or thrust control levers, are set during flight operations. In autopilot mode, movement is automatic. *Jakoeb Vandahlen / US Navy*

Adm. Harry Harris Jr., commander of the US Pacific Fleet, observes during a RIMPAC 2014 ISR flight. He is occupying the cockpit jump seat position. *David Kolmel / US Navy*

While on a deployment to Australia with VP-16, Lt. Kenneth Savage preflights his P-8A before a flight to search for signs of Malaysian Airlines flight MH370. *Keith DeVinney / US Navy*

P-8A Naval Aircrewman (Operator) 2nd Class Karl Shinn looks intently for any sign of MH370, which vanished without a trace. He is at the port observer window. *Keith DeVinney / US Navy*

When contacts are **spotted**, the observer takes digital photos to create a record of the operation. The large window offers many options for picture opportunities. *Jakoeb Vandahlen / US Navy*

P-8A observers scan the sea for Malaysian Airlines flight MH370. In this setting, the cabin lighting is dimmed so that glare on the windows is kept to a minimum. *Keith DeVinney / US Navy*

Flying over the Indian Ocean in April 2014, Chief Naval Aircrewman Samuel Judd of VP-16 scans the surface, binoculars at the ready the instant he sees something out of the ordinary. *Keith DeVinney / US Navy*

Florida senator Marco Rubio tours a P-8A at NAS Jacksonville with VP-16 commanding officer Molly Boron. Visits like these keep lawmakers aware of funding priorities. *Gulianna Dunn / US Navy*

The Royal Saudi naval forces are shown a P-8A rotary sonobuoy launcher by Lt. Fan Yang of VP-5. Saudi Arabia has shown interest in purchasing P-8A aircraft. *Jakoeb Vandahlen / US Navy*

Capt. Scott Dillon shows Admiral Jonathan Greenert, chief of naval operations, the P-8A in July 2014. This area is where the mission operators work. *Peter D. Lawlor / US Navy*

Foreign attaché officers are shown the P-8A by Lt. Josh Lowery of Patrol and Recon Wing 11. Allies appreciate such briefings and views into US capabilities. *Clark Pierce / US Navy*

CHAPTER 4
Exterior Details

Following is a detailed review of the P-8A Poseidon exterior features and unique items. From a distance, the plane could nearly pass for a Boeing 737 series of commercial airliner. Getting closer, you see military markings and note such details as there being few windows, with plenty of bumps, fairings, and antennas all over. The wings sport pylons. There are labels and warning stencils everywhere. It is then apparent that this variant of the successful passenger transport is truly a distinct breed. The Navy made a wise choice adapting this proven and capable aircraft, saving much time and taxpayer dollars as opposed to creating a brand-new type, which would have involved years and millions of dollars in development and testing cycles.

It has a larger interior space than is in the P-3C, has two fewer engines, and has proven able to adapt to major alterations such as incorporating a weapons bay and underwing stores equipment. Most important is the potential for the P-8A to add more upgrades and components over time, something the P-3C was no longer able to accommodate.

The plane must also be able to include many other systems, such as the electro-optical sensor turret, an ESM array, naval radar, and missile-warning systems. Also installed was a DIRCM turret and data-link capability. All of this and much more has been built into the aircraft, with space intentionally left open for even more gear as time and tactics progress and technology advances.

The P-8A aircrew works in comfort, in a cabin designed so that crew coordination and teamwork are enhanced. In the P-3C, station operators were physically separated, which was a weakness in fluid situations to quickly comprehend the big picture of many unfolding event elements. The P-8A eliminates much of that, since the five operator stations are all in one section of the cabin layout. Crew members can also view everything that any of the others are looking at and working on. This increases effective inputs to mission challenges and improves results by several orders of magnitude.

P-8A Poseidon, BuNo 168434, starboard nose profile. Radome houses APY-10 radar. RESCUE arrow shows where to open sliding cockpit window. ESM/RWR are to left of 434. *Author*

P-8A, BuNo 168434, port angle shows pitot static system probe above angle-of-attack probe by numeral 4. Black coating on radome protects nose from excessive surface erosion. *Author*

This is about the only angle that reveals little of the P-8A, other than the Buzz number. The internal airstair is shown here deployed. *Juan S. Sua/US Navy*

Aft of nose on right side are a pair of pitot static air inlet heated probes, which feed air to various flight systems. The angle-of-attack probe moves to indicate dive/climb maneuvers. *Author*

P-8A, BuNo 168434, nose view shows flat gray-painted section above the cockpit windows. This prevents the flying-boom operator from sun reflections when connecting. *Author*

Left side shows air temperature indicator below the "4": an ice detector probe is under the ESM fairing. Airstair is stowed inside the rectangular door under normal entry door. *Author*

Just aft of the nose radome is a small blade antenna, part of the ALQ-240 ESM (electronic support measures) system. *Author*

A view of the left-hand gear door shows a red towing-limit warning, and the ALE-47 CMDS safety switch pin location. *Author*

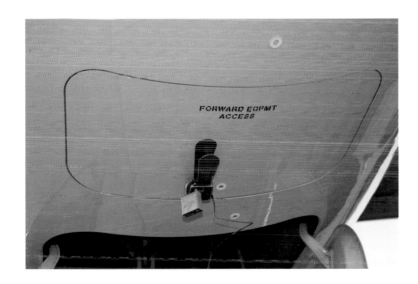

FORWARD EQPMT ACCESS

Just ahead of the nose landing gear is this door, which allows access to forward avionics "black boxes" such as radar and navigation equipment. *Author*

Inside the nose landing-gear bay, at the forward end of the right corner, is the ALE-47 safety pin housing. This removes electric power to the modules. *Author*

P-8A Poseidon nose landing gear (NLG) arrangement, with dual wheels. A powerful taxi lamp is between the tires to give the aircrew maximum visibility low to the ground when moving around an airfield at night. *Author*

The P-8A complies with all federal standards, including the use of traffic alert and collision avoidance system (TCAS) gear. This AT-910 antenna is a part of the equipment fit. It is located just aft of the NLG bay section. *Author*

The forward section of the nose landing-gear bay reveals this pair of snubbers on the top bulkhead. They are used to stop rotation of the nosewheels/tires after they are pulled into the bay for stowage on takeoff. They rub against the tire surfaces, slowing them down at first, then stopping them from spinning. They hold the tires in place until landing, when the gear assembly is lowered. The round cylinder with red border is a ground crew warning horn. To far right (*center*) is a lamp used to provide illumination inside the bay for inspections and work done in darkness. *Author*

As one moves farther down the left side, a warning stripe showing engine ingestion area, an airstair-operating panel, and a small floodlight are seen. *Author*

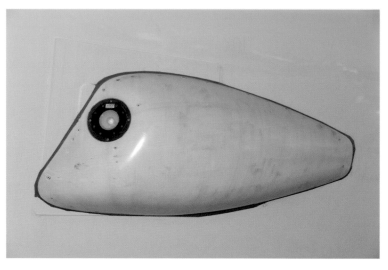

This fairing on the left side contains the AAR-54 passive missile approach warning sensor. It stares into a 90-degree sector of airspace, alerting the aircrew if a hot missile plume is detected. *Author*

Early P-8As were delivered with the AAR-54 PMAWS (passive missile approach warning system) devices. Yellow tag reads "WINDOW MAY BE HOT." *Author*

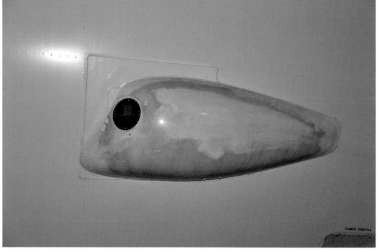

This sensor is an advanced missile plume detector, part of the LAIRCM system. It detects missiles approaching in the ultraviolet and infrared (UV/IR) bandwidths and feeds data to the AAQ-24 DIRCM turret. *Author*

P-8A, BuNo 168763, shows more left-hand features, including the electrically deployed airstair. This folds flat and retracts into the fuselage. With this device, the P-8A is less dependent on ground-based equipment when operating from austere locations. Nose radome houses APY-10 multimode radar and surveillance antennas. Just above the large ESM fairing is a small, round aerial enclosed within a rectangular panel. This is a radar warning receiver or RWR. The white swept-blade antenna on the spine of the fuselage is a VHF antenna. Aft of this is a UHF antenna. The two white-winged antennas aft of the observer's window are a pair of satcom (satellite communication) antennas. *Author*

P-8A self-defense equipment includes these four ALE-47 modules containing thirty rounds of flares, used to lure away infrared guided missiles. A blanking plate covers the empty bay. *Author*

Krueger flaps are along the underside of the wing. Above these are high-intensity landing/taxiing illuminating lamps. Engine nacelle is barely visible to right. *Author*

A NACA-section ram air intake is at the left-wing root section. It takes in outside air to cool electrical equipment. The ram air inlet deflector door is closed. *Author*

Newer-production P-8As have this LED (light-emitting diode) type of lighting for taxiing and takeoff/landing. They emit a more balanced distribution of light, using less power. *Author*

The P-8A has a pair of CFM56-7B (2X) engines. Cowl inlet lips are heated to prevent ice buildup. Thrust reversers are used to slow down after landing. Fairing houses 180 kilovolt-ampere (kVA) generator. *Author*

Aviation Electronics Tech. Victor French of VP-26 "Tridents" performs a postflight engine oil check. Normal engine oil consumption per hour is 25.6 ounces. *Sean R. Morton / US Navy*

A view inside shows the engine nacelle inner wall (*right*) with blades, and, *to left*, the engine itself. In a high-bypass design, the first blade stage directs air around the engine, to cool it and reduce noise. *Author*

A fan blade loop inspection is undertaken by Aviation Machinist's Mate 2nd Class Miko Brandon of VP-4. These are first-stage blades of wide chord, attached to the disk by clips. *Juan S. Sua / US Navy*

A CFM-series engine on display at the Farnborough Airshow in 2010. The gray tank mounted on the outer engine case is for lubricating oil. Numerous accessory drives are mounted below it, as are electronic units such as the EEC (engine electronic controller) or a FADEC (fuel and digital engine control) or both. These "black boxes" run the engine at optimum performance while regulating fuel flow for best economic benefit. Between the outer engine case and inner engine core is where the excess high-bypass air flows. The inner core compresses the incoming airflow. The air is then injected with a fuel mist that is ignited. The aft, or "hot," section is where the hot exhaust gases are expelled, rotating the exhaust blades. Various engine "stages" supply bleed air to accessories. The fifth and ninth stages pass air by means of a regulating valve to the ECS (environmental control system), used for cabin and avionics bay air conditioning, as an example. *Author*

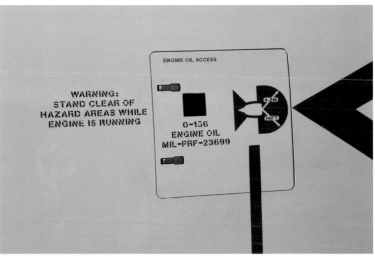

P-8A, BuNo 169340, left number 1 engine, with the first-stage fan blades visible. Swirled line spins when fans are rotating. Air inlet temperature probe is at ten o'clock position. *Author*

The engine oil access door also shows engine ingestion areas. The area in red, 4.2 meters (14 feet) in an arc around the intake, should be avoided with the engine running. *Author*

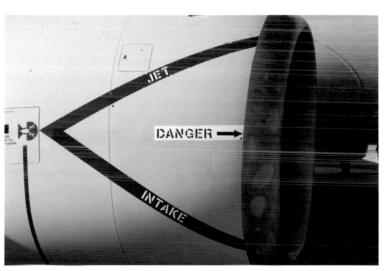

A strake is here on the inboard side of the engine nacelle. It directs airflow, reducing turbulence, in order to improve lift and flight control. Both nacelles have this feature. *Author*

A red chevron stripe on both sides of the nacelle forward end provide a distinct visual warning of engine turbine inlets. A bleed air duct blowout panel is near the word "JET." *Author*

P-8A, BuNo 169340, inside a hangar at NAS Jacksonville has the port (*left*) number 1 engine cowling access panels open for maintenance. Two prop rods hold the curved panel away from the actual engine itself. The large generator fairing overlaps the forward cowling panel when closed. The low height of the nacelle allows for easy access to everything in this outboard section. The open panel is of composite construction. Sheets of carbon fiber are laid into a mold; a liquid resin is applied, then dried. The panel is then trimmed, sanded, and painted. *Author*

A view of the outboard engine section shows the integrated drive generator (IDG) at lower left. It provides a constant level of electric current, regardless of engine rpm. *Author*

The inboard section of number 1 engine shows, *at top*, the gray FFC, which can also be called a FADEC unit. Outer case design aids in heat rejection. Black oil reservoir is below. *Author*

Engine number 1, aft view of nacelle, shows the exhaust duct and lower pylon features. Slender tube extending aft out of the pylon itself is a drain that allows excess fuel or hydraulic fluid that accumulates inside the lower pylon interior to vent overboard. The lower pylon surfaces, as well as the inner engine exhaust, are composed of an exotic metal called Inconel, which is extremely heat resistant. It has been used in several experimental aircraft programs such as the X-15. The aft cowl outer sections move aft, exposing rows of vanes called cascades. They force air in a forward direction, using reverse thrust to slow the plane down on the runway after landing. *Author*

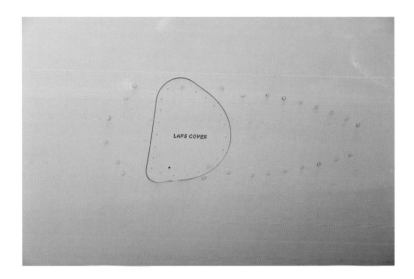

Under the observer's window, left side, is this access for LAPS, the liquid air palletized system. This is a nonhinged panel, held in place with screws. *Author*

The left outer-wing station in this photo shows the pylon fairing and bomb release unit (BRU)-76. C-clamp-looking devices are sway braces, to keep munitions from rocking side to side. *Author*

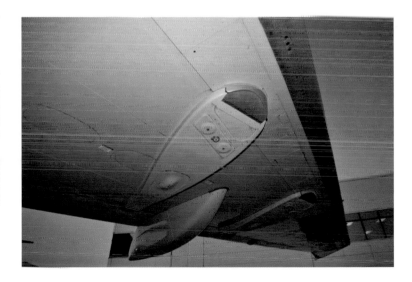

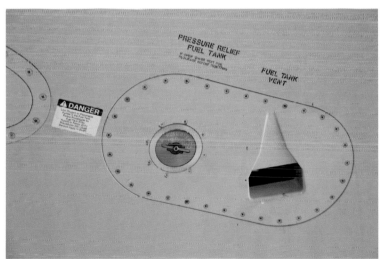

The underside of the left wing is where two weapon station hardpoints are located. The leading edge is deiced. This view shows the mount without the pylon fairing or rack unit. *Author*

Under the wing are two fuel-related items: the fuel tank vent, fed by ram air to reduce fume buildup, and the pressure relief, a manually operated valve, used before removing panels. *Author*

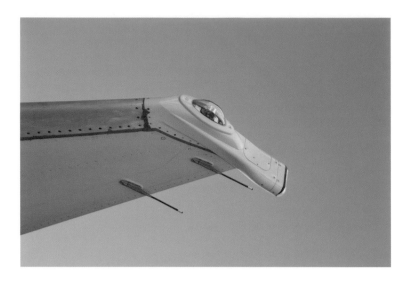

At the end of the raked wingtips are an anticollision strobe light and two static wicks or dischargers. As an aircraft builds up an electrical charge, these dissipate the energy. *Author*

The left main wheel well of a P-8A. Wheels/tires are exposed to the slipstream, and rubber seals prevent turbulent air from entering the bay. Hydraulic fluid accumulator is the round tank. *Author*

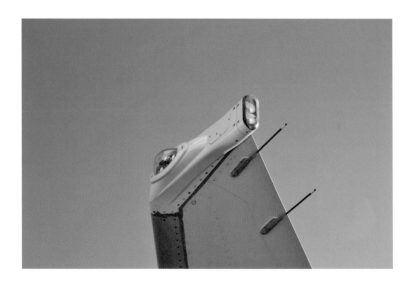

Another angle shows this position light. It glows steadily, projecting light aft, whereas the anticollision beams are oriented outboard. They are cooled by airflow. *Author*

Another view inside this bay shows a pair of white attitude level indicators. The one at the bottom of the hydraulic reservoir shows pitch. The other shows roll, fixed to aft bulkhead. *Author*

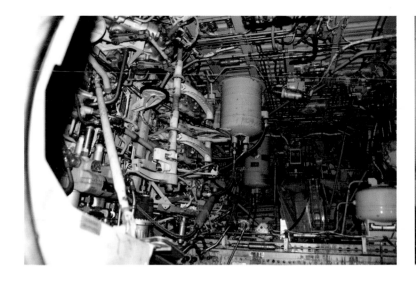

P-8A main landing-gear wells are a mass of tubes, arms, hoses, pulleys, wires, and cylinders. Three large hydraulic fluid tanks dominate the view looking to starboard/right. *Author*

Aft of the left wing root is this ALE-47 dispenser housing. A pair on each side allows for a total of 120 rounds of MJU-50 flares to be carried and used if need be. *Author*

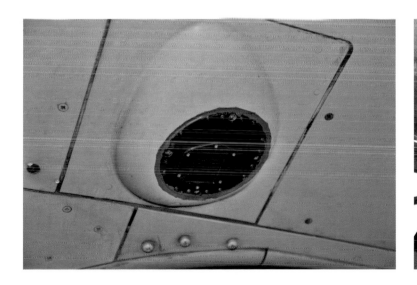

This UV/IR missile-warning sensor stares straight down, just aft of the left main wheel well. It keeps watch below the flight path of the aircraft, to detect a missile rising up to attack it. *Author*

These two fairings just forward of the main gear wells cover attachment hardpoints for bomb racks, or as aft mounts for the APS-154 radar. *Author*

The left main landing-gear assembly of a P-8A. Dual wheels and tires are attached to an air/oil shock strut that works just like shocks on an automobile. *Author*

A close-up view of the hub assembly shows brakes, the feed line for hydraulic brake fluid, and the line that connects to brake caliper, compressed when pilots use the brake pedals. *Author*

Side view of a main landing gear. Tire grooves are designed to shed water when landings are made on wet runways. Tires are filled with nitrogen gas instead of air. *Author*

A maintenance crew of VP-4 "Skinny Dragons" performs a tire change, exposing the brake discs. The rotors spin; the stators are fixed. These press against each other, stopping the plane. *Juan S. Sua / US Navy*

A view of the midsection of the lower fuselage shows three identical swept-blade antennas. These detect signals from deployed sonobuoys, part of the sonobuoy positioning system or SPS array. *To left*, what appears to be another antenna is in fact stenciled "FUEL SHROUD AND HYDRAULIC DRAIN," known as a drain mast. The large radome contains OBIGGS (onboard inert gas–generating system) gear, and also the ALQ-240 ESM scanner. This is a spinning array of antennas, used to detect signals of tactical/intelligence value. Coverage is a constant 360 degrees as the aircraft flies. The five stripes are for lightning energy dissipation. At far right is a small black aerial. This detects radar signals striking the bottom of the aircraft, part of the radar-warning receiver (RWR) suite. *Author*

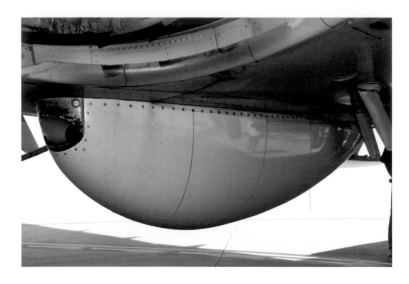

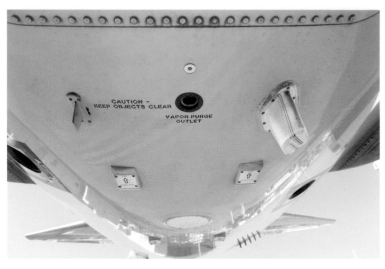

A quarter-angle view of the ESM/OBIGGS radome. Air inlet is to supply air for OBIGGS inert-gas mixture to be pumped into fuel tanks. ESM scanner occupies most of the space. *Author*

Continuing aft, there are these two antennas. The yellow one is for MIDS (multifunctional information distribution system), and the right one is a command data link (CDL) omni. *Author*

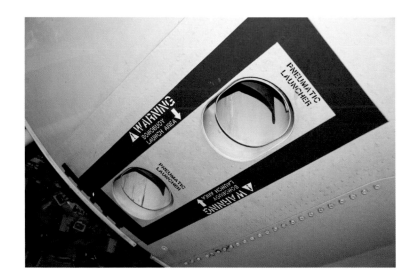

Aft of the weapons bay is this dual sonobuoy tube launch area. It is marked with a 3-inch red border, meeting FS 11136. *Author*

This array is an LRRA (low-range radio altimeter). It provides an accurate indication of height above the ground or sea surface. Central element emits signal; four square ones receive it. *Author*

A wide-angle view of the left-aft fuselage section shows many features. The large, slender fairing is a radome housing the common data-link antenna for reception on the port side. Inside is a steerable dish antenna that moves in order to maintain a signal. The system automatically switches between antennas (the one seen here, the omni below, and the identical steerable one on the other side) to preserve the integrity of signal lock. To the right is a single sonobuoy pneumatic launcher tube. Pneumatic (air) pressure is used to propel the buoys clear of the aircraft. At the lower left are closed weapon bay doors. *Author*

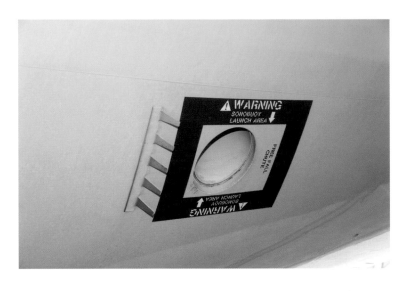

The free-fall chute uses no pressure to drop sonobuoys. The five-bladed strip ahead of the chute is an air deflector, used to reduce slipstream airflow intensity at the opening. *Author*

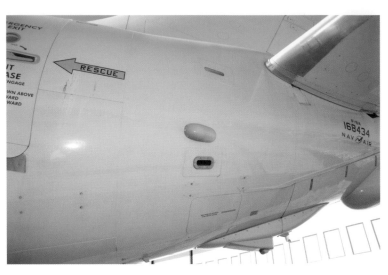

Small ESM array is inside radome. Panel below is stenciled "SECTION 48 ACCESS AND BLOWOUT DOOR." Slotted vents above/below ESM fairing are cooling-air intake/exhaust. *Author*

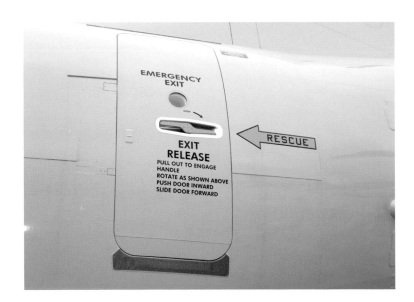

On the P-8A, this door is used as an emergency exit, and also as a maintenance access to the cabin. The metal strip at the bottom reinforces the edge against heavy-object damage. *Author*

Aviation Structural Mechanics 1st Class Melvin Ascuncion, *left*, and Av. Struct. Mech. 2nd Class Efhril Elomina work on the left horizontal stabilator. *Juan S. Sua / US Navy*

P-8A, BuNo 169335, data plate is riveted near the left stabilator. The manufacturer's model number is 737-800A. The MSN or manufacturer's serial number is 63183. *Author*

The lower pod of the tail cone houses the LAIRCM turret, AAR-54 PMAWS in this image, and ALQ-240 ESM arrays. The two outlets are for the air eductor (*above*) and APU. *Author*

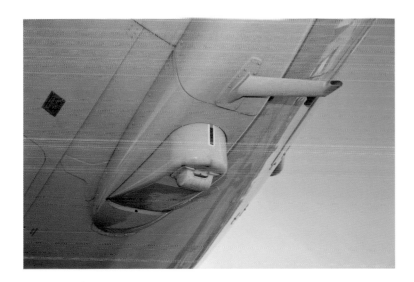

The tail skid is seen here. It prevents damage if the plane is overrotated on takeoff or landing. A pressurized strut cushions ground contact. Green shows good pressure. *Author*

The AAQ-24 large-aircraft infrared countermeasures (LAIRCM) turret is cued by data from AAR-54 or updated UV/IR sensors. It then emits a pulsed, intense energy beam at missiles. *Author*

The P-8A tail cone contains extensive equipment for many purposes. The small outlet at the very top is the air eductor exhaust. The larger exhaust below this is for the auxiliary power unit. Below the exhausts is the lower support pod housing ALQ-240 ESM fixed arrays for monitoring the aft sectors as the aircraft flies. The round sensors are AAR-54 passive missile approach warning units, replaced on newer P-8As by UV/IR devices. These detect and pass data to the gray turret below, the AAQ-24 LAIRCM hardware. Fully articulated, the turret optics aim at the approaching missile and fire a beam of focused, intense, coded pulses. This overwhelms the missile seeker, causing it to miss. Around the turret are four cooling vents, for the electronic gear. *Author*

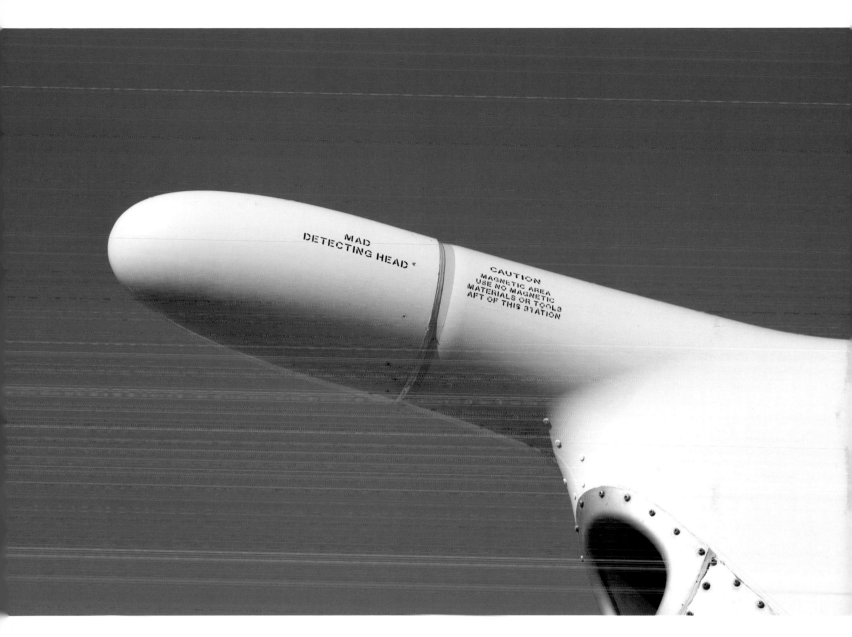

P-8A Poseidon, BuNo 168428, shows the magnetic-anomaly detector (MAD) detecting-head housing. It is located at the very aft end of the tail cone and is a prominent recognition feature attached to ASW aircraft that seek out underwater vessels lurking in the ocean depths. Such large objects as submarines disturb the natural magnetic fields generated by the earth as they move about. Known magnetic patterns stored in the MAD software are compared to those showing irregularities in search sectors. These can reveal general locations where a sub may be present, but further investigation by using sonobuoys would be the next step to confirm and locate a suspected contact. *Author*

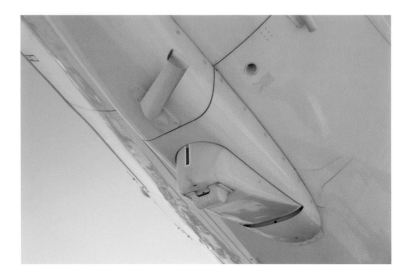

This view shows the fuel dump pipe and, to the right, a hole with a symbol showing where to place one of a number of floor jacks in order to raise the aircraft off the ground. *Author*

Overall view of the lower empennage section. The stabilator moves and has a heated leading edge to keep it ice free. The ESM radome is below the air intake. BuNo is stenciled on both sides. *Author*

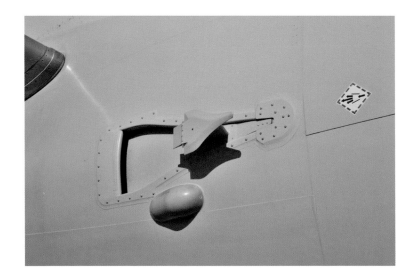

Now, as one moves along the right side of the fuselage, ahead of the stabilator, is the NACA-section air intake for APU and eductor. The diamond placard indicates an air intake. *Author*

P-8A, BuNo 168434, of VP-45, tail fin has "Pelicans" artwork adorning right side. "LN" is used by the squadron as its tail code. An elevator feel system probe is below the pelican beak. *Author*

Contained within the tail fin is an INMARSAT antenna. This area is also where the top rudder hinge is located, as well as several electric-static dischargers. *Author*

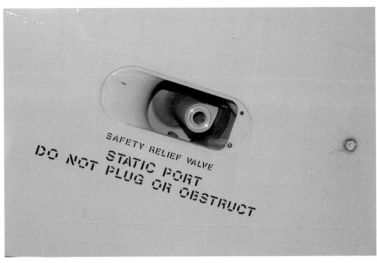

One of a pair of safety relief valves by the powered outflow valve. These protect the cabin, venting air if an overpressure condition occurs. It is set to vent at 8.95 psi. *Author*

This cutaway view shows a fairing of a tail-fin tip, with an antenna design much like the AMT-50 in use. It can track a satellite by means of a fully articulated mounting. *Author*

Similar to the left side is this arrangement of ESM radome and sonobuoy pneumatic launchers. Along the bottom are LRRA, MIDS, and CDL antennas. *Author*

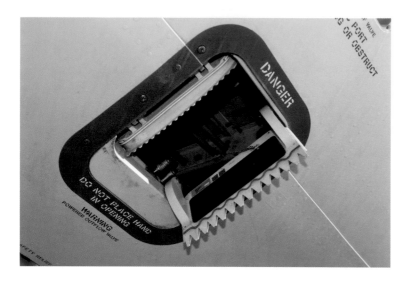

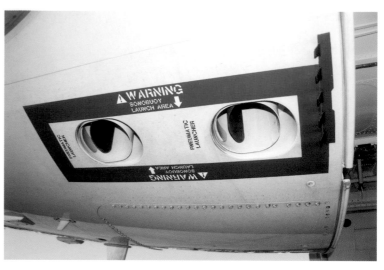

Below the safety relief valve is this powered outflow valve. It regulates the cabin pressure during flight to maintain the equivalent of air pressure at 8,000 feet. *Author*

These dual launcher tubes are connected to the cabin rotary launchers. The dark guides ensure that the buoy does not hang up along the tube walls as it falls. Weapon bay is to right. *Author*

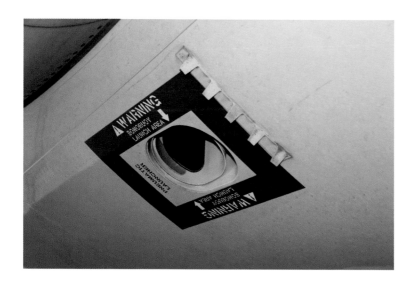

Another single sonobuoy pneumatic launcher is below the right-side CDL fairing. All buoy loading is done internally. The angle that is shown is looking back toward the tail. *Author*

Right-side view of open weapons-bay doors. Doors fold from centerline to outboard, hinged into two sections. This provides for an open, unobstructed bay space for five pylons. *Author*

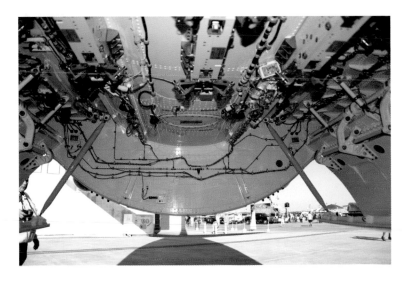

P-8A, BuNo 168434, weapons bay, seen looking aft. Arms supporting bay door corners are seen; racks where ordnance can be hung are at the top of image. *Author*

The left doors are seen here from inside the bay, looking outboard. Above the doors are wires, fluid lines, and plugs for electrical-interface connections. *Author*

A view looking forward shows aft shape of ESM/OBIGGS radome, pylon station control units, and door actuator linkages. Weapons loaded here all face forward. *Author*

This left-aft corner shows the in-line motors that move the doors open or closed. Doors are made as light as possible, but strong enough to withstand aerodynamic buffeting. *Author*

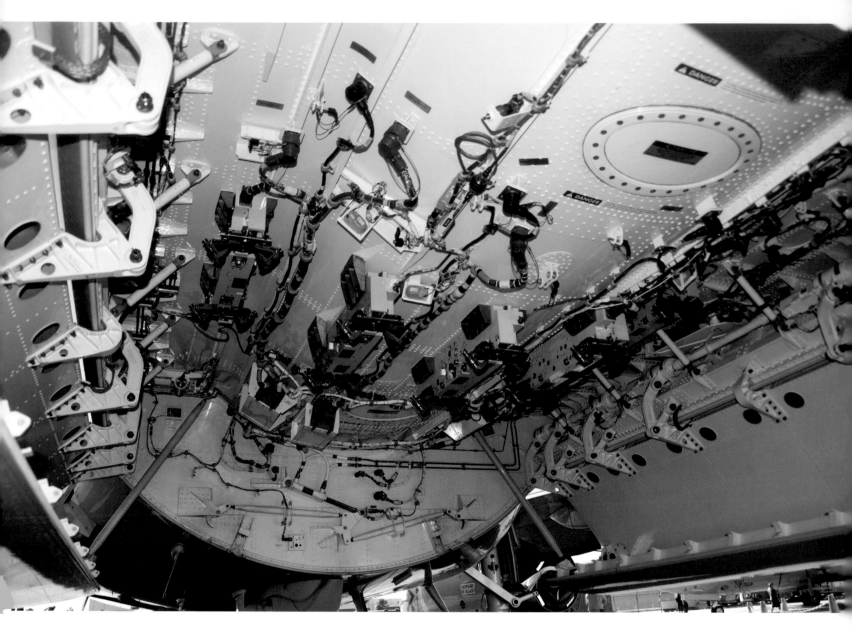

P-8A Poseidon, BuNo 168434, weapons-bay view, looking forward. There are five pylons, designated BRU-75. They are numbered from left to right, stations 5 through 9. These racks are of the pneumatic-release type. Most pylon racks jettison their weapons by using pyrotechnic cartridges; these need cleaning to remove soot and grime after each mission. The pneumatic systems are air operated, so they need no cleaning. Electrical wires with plugs, when not in use, are stored in sockets, as seen here. The white paint that is used makes it much easier to spot any fluid leaks or scorch marks from a shorted circuit. The Mk. 54 torpedo or Mk. 62 Quickstrike mine is carried in this space, as is a search-and-rescue UNI-PAC II air-dropped survival kit. *Author*

A Mk. 54 lightweight torpedo is raised to be attached to the number 7 pylon. A live weapon is shown by the yellow band around the warhead section. A shroud protects the propellers, and a rubber cap protects the nose sonar transducer as the uploading occurs. A crewman has an open procedures manual, checking by reading off the steps it takes to perform this operation. Location is at Ault Field, on Whidbey Island in Washington State. The squadron at work is of VP-4, the "Skinny Dragons." The fixed-wing-launched version of this torpedo weighs 645 pounds (292.6 kg), is 113.2 inches (2.87 m) long, and has a diameter of 12.75 inches (324 mm). The warhead contains polymer-based explosives (PBXN-103) weighing 96.8 pounds (43.9 kg). The torpedo can travel at speeds up to 46 miles per hour (74.1 km per hour), powered by Otto II liquid fuel. *Juan S. Sua / US Navy*

Various safety items in the weapons-bay section include these bright 28-volt lamps to provide ample light during work in hours of darkness. *Author*

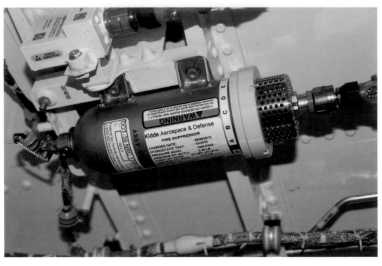

These cylinders contain a halon agent that chemically prevents fires from spreading. Perforated nozzle sprays in a 360-degree arc. *Author*

A fire in this compartment would have serious results, so these optical fire detectors monitor the bay and will alert the crew while activating the fire suppression system. *Author*

Four of these large placards outside the doors provide instructions to take before any inside work begins. Red paint is of FS 11136. *Author*

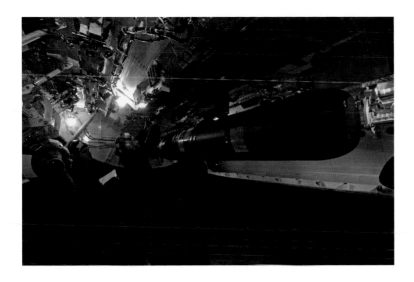

One of the many predeployment qualification phases involves this night loading of a practice Mk. 54 torpedo. Illumination of the bay streamlines teamwork results. *Juan S. Sua / US Navy*

Reverse angle of BRU-75 racks, showing two suspension hooks, spaced at 14 inches. They rotate open, one of a series of actions used in the dropping of ordnance. *Author*

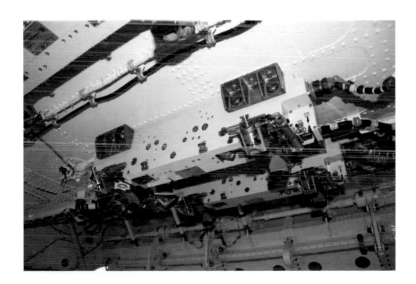

Detail view of the BRU-75 racks in a P-8A weapons bay. The air pressure operating range is from 3,800 to 5,999 psi. Racks are bolted into the brackets of the upper-bay deck. *Author*

In this close-up image, the controls and settings are seen. The white power knob, vent valve, pressure gauge, hook position, and manual release all are visible. *Author*

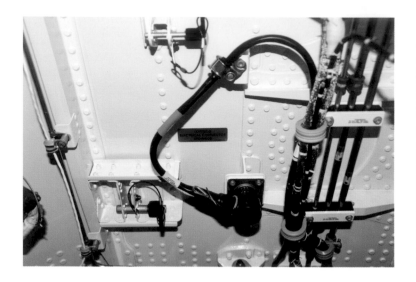

When torpedoes are not present, their associated cannon plugs and wires are safely stowed as shown, to prevent them from hanging loosely and swinging about. *Author*

Station control units 8 and 9 are located near the forward-bay bulkhead. They interface with the weapon on each rack, providing update inputs and release commands. *Author*

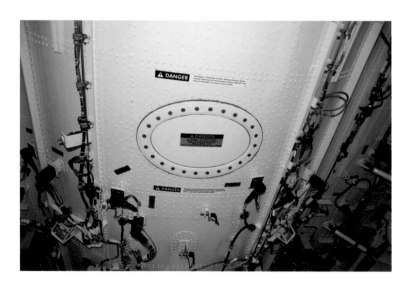

Access to the aft fuel tanks is done from the weapons bay. This view shows one access cover; also seen are safety pin and various electric plug stowage sockets. *Author*

Weapons-bay control unit number 10, enclosed inside this protective compartment. Plugs are of the quick-disconnect design, two clamps are loosened, and the unit slides out. *Author*

Continuing along the right (starboard) side of the aircraft, moving forward, is this view of the ESM/OBIGGS radome, with ALE-47 chaff/flare module 2B. Were the module installed, thirty circular holes containing MJU-50 flare cartridges would be seen. The blade antenna below this is another SPS (sonobuoy positioning system) aerial. The white blade at right is a combination of very high-frequency, ultrahigh frequency, IFF (identification friend or foe), and air traffic control (VHF-UHF-IFF-ATC) antenna. The large panel inboard of the white-bladed antenna is marked as "GROUND MAINTENANCE PANEL INSIDE—AFT AUX TANK SUMP DRAIN." The low-profile white antenna below CMDS is used to capture signals from a ground-based marker beacon. *Author*

P-8A, BuNo 168433, opened ground maintenance panel. The arrangement of this section includes insulated plumbing and a large tank that is an air separation module. The round, red-rubber seal with a motor is an air extraction device to force hot air overboard. The switch panel by the door hinges has a pin-blocking operation of two switches. These isolate electric current to the weapons-bay doors and must be pinned before anyone can work inside the bay section. *Author*

P-8A, BuNo 169004, in the process of being decorated with a VP-4 "Skinny Dragons" emblem by Aviation Structural Mechanics 2nd Class Ricardo Mendoza and Efhril Elomina. *Juan S. Sua / US Navy*

This view of a right main landing-gear strut shows the gear well panels fastened to the strut. The plane has evidently been to Canada, as this "zap" marking plainly shows! *Author*

APU access is via the large panel forward of the lower tail-cone pod. It is essentially a small turbine engine that provides power in flight and on the ground. *Juan S. Sua / US Navy*

Another view inside the complicated main wheel bays from the right side. Just to the left of the lower hydraulic tank are the controls to operate or shut down the APU. *Author*

This large access door is hinged along the right side. Releasing the three clamps lowers the panel to expose the auxiliary power unit (APU). The space is cooled by an air eductor, which also cools the oil. The tailplane support truss structure is also accessed in this area. A titanium-lined firewall is at the forward end of the compartment. The long, angled tube is the fuel vent. Part of the aft section of the panel is the aft lower-pod fairing of the tail cone, which contains elements of the ALQ-240 ESM system and the directional infrared countermeasures turret. *Author*

Located on the aft bulkhead, in the starboard MLG bay, is this area for operation of the APU in case of a fire in that section. The round device is an audible warning horn. *Author*

These two spheres are pressure cylinders containing halon fire-suppression agent. A pyrotechnic squib fires to release the fluid if a fire occurs in the MLG bay. *Author*

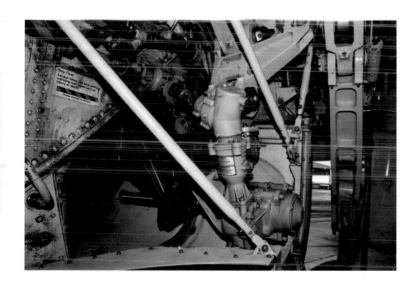

The green device is the left flap actuator and transmission, which lowers/raises the inboard wing flap into the slipstream. The jackscrew can be seen pointing aft. *Author*

The starboard MLG bay, viewed from the port MLG bay, shows the main gear trunnion; the large tank to the left is a 10.7-US-gallon reservoir for hydraulic system B. *Author*

P-8A, BuNo 168428, right-wing fairings contain the double-slotted Fowler-type flap actuators. Constructed of carbon fiber, they are lightweight, aerodynamic shapes. *Author*

Left-wing underside has the word "NAVY" in 36-inch-high letters. FS 17038 black paint is used to provide a definitive contrast for identification purposes. *Author*

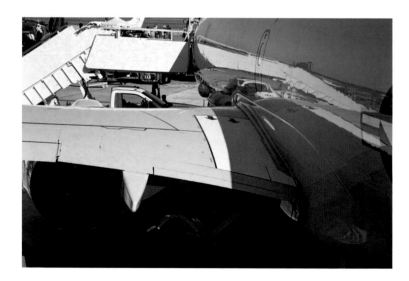

In the event the cabin crew has to use the overwing exits, the egress area is of a nonskid surface, with arrows that show the path to the wing trailing edge. *Author*

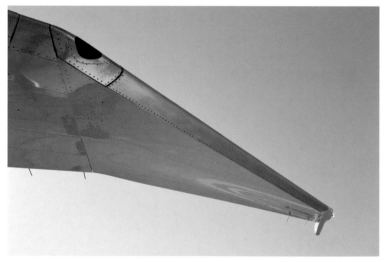

The red navigation light shows that this is the left raked wingtip. On the right wing, a green light is present. These tips do not fold and are made of composite materials. *Author*

The undersides of both wings have these multiple access panels, which can be removed to do work inside the fuel cells. The wing leading edge is toward the top side of the image. *Author*

Forward of the right wing is another LAPS equipment access panel, oval shaped and screwed into the fuselage. A sealing gasket is applied to the inner edge. *Author*

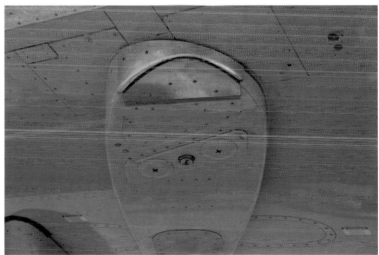

The old plug-type overwing exit hatches, which a person had to pull into the cabin and discard. New exits are hinged to move up and out of the way of egress paths. *Author*

The inboard right-wing hardpoint fairing is shown here; the leading edge is reinforced against damage and is heated to prevent ice from accumulating. *Author*

P-8A, BuNo 168434; wide-angle picture of the starboard-side fuselage shows wing root and NACA-section inlet that draws in outside air used for cooling electrical components and distributed for other uses. The large door below the observer's window allows access to avionics and batteries. An ALE-47 countermeasures dispenser is to the right of the avionics bay door. The lack of windows results in a stronger fuselage, with a lot fewer holes cut out of it. The overall fuselage itself is designed in the "double-bubble" cross section, an extremely durable configuration. *Author*

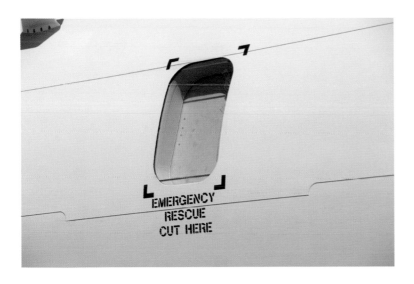

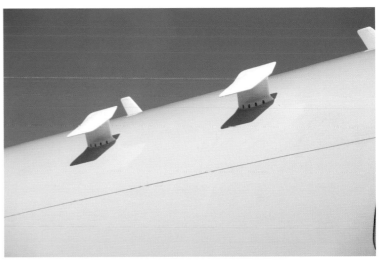

The right observer's window, heated to prevent mist and frost from forming. Cut-in area is designed by the manufacturer as an area clear of fuel/hydraulic lines, wires, and cables. *Author*

Both upper sides have a pair of batwing satcom antennas. The two pairs allow for redundancy and provide for many frequencies to be accessed simultaneously. *Author*

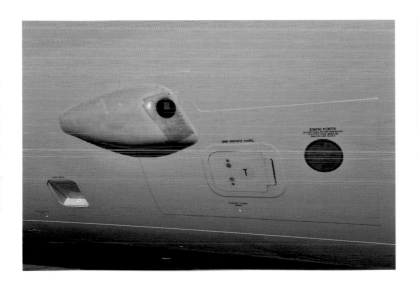

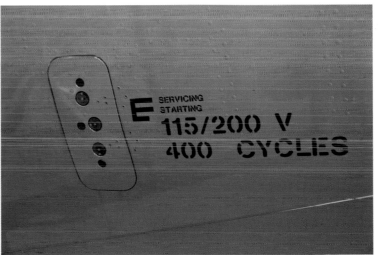

Shown here in detail are, *from left*, ALE-47, fairing for UV/IR MWS sensor, the ground-servicing panel, lavatory vents, and a bare-aluminum static vent area. *Author*

If a P-8A needs external power, this panel is opened so that a large power cord can be plugged in. The plane can also be started if the APU is not used or is not in service. *Author*

Stored inside this closed pair of doors is the MX-20 ultra-long-range, multisensor/multispectral turret. Enclosing the device within the fuselage prevents damage to the delicate optical surfaces from debris thrown up from a landing or takeoff. This also reduces aerodynamic-drag effects when not used, which influences fuel economy and range. In addition to use as a surveillance tool, another benefit is observing wing pylon–mounted stores, weapons-bay drops, and engine performance. *Author*

The MX-20 turret provides a passive-sensing capability, instead of using radar, to find objects that emit radio frequency waves that can be detected by hostile forces. The turret views scenes on land or at sea in visible wavelengths the human eye can sense, and in the infrared (IR) bandwidth, which is useful at night. The IR bands are also useful for detecting differences in heat intensity day or night. For example, a P-8A can fly alongside an underway cargo ship and determine via infrared wavelengths which holds contain cargo and which are empty. The turret weighs 200 pounds fully equipped, with up to seven sensors. Tilt range is +90 to –120 degrees. A 2-megapixel high-definition zoom/spotter camera provides 1080-pixel resolution. Five-axis stabilization consisting of three-axis inner (pitch/roll/yaw) and two-axis outer (azimuth/elevation) results in image scenes with stable, legible views in most situations. Fields of view (FOV) at 1080 pixels include 0.92, 0.46, 0.29, and 0.17 degrees. Naval Aircrewman (Operator) 2nd Class Mike Burnett of VP-16 wipes down the optical surfaces of a lowered MX-20 turret in readiness for a flight to hunt for signs of Malaysian Airlines flight MH370. *Eric A. Pastor / US Navy*

Naval Aircrewman (Operator) 3rd Class Jonathan Zaminski of VP-45 uses the MX-20 sensor to view action during a SINKEX (sinking exercise) in September 2018. The SINKEX was one part of the Valiant Shield 2018 event. Old ships no longer in service are towed out to deep waters, where warships, aircraft, and submarines can participate in live-fire drills. These actions enhance crew morale, while putting procedures into practice that would be used in a wartime scenario. The image is an infrared view as the ship absorbs hits from a large munition. *Seth Rosenberg / US Marine Corps*

CHAPTER 5
Interior Details

The P-8A Poseidon has an interior layout much improved over that of the P-3C Orion. On the flight deck, the two occupants have a comprehensive electronic flight instrumentation system or EFIS "Glass" cockpit suite, making their workload much less and reducing fatigue factors. The pilot enjoys a HUD (head-up display) that projects symbology related to flight and mission data, keeping eyes outside and viewing the airspace instead of constantly shifting between the instruments and the view through the windows. The observers' job is made much easier by the use of large, heated windows and being seated in comfort as they scan beneath them on SAR missions. The five operators have at their fingertips many options, from ESM assessments to weapons status, radar imagery, and visual capabilities of the MX-20 sensor turret. They can work together in critical situations or divide up the workload of many facets among themselves.

Sonobuoy loading and management are much improved in a space logically laid out for the tasks. Storage, loading, and deployment require less effort and planning.

The end result of taking advantage of strides in the electronics field, ergonomic realities, and sensible configuration practices makes today's P-8A vastly more capable to perform the many mission assignments it is called on to carry out.

P-8A, BuNo 169335, cockpit windows. The main windshields have a sealed coating, two thermally tempered glass sheets separated by an interlayer of urethane to resist delamination. *Author*

This is a HUD view from inside a Boeing Business Jet. Flight data glows in green symbols, such as airspeed, artificial horizon, altitude, heading, and waypoints. The pilot can concentrate on the outside world. *Author*

P-8A Poseidon, BuNo 169335, flight deck. HUD image combiner glass is lowered and is provided only for the pilot / aircraft commander, who sits at left-hand seat. Five large multifunction displays do away with past decades of rows of round-dial mechanical gauges. Center display primarily shows engine-operating features such as turbine rpm, exhaust gas temperature (EGT), fuel flow, and internal temperatures. Both aircrew have two displays in front of them, which they can set to show flight images such as artificial horizon, overlaid with readouts essential to observe for flying operations. They can also view, on the central lower display, images from the MX-20 sensor, or tactical maps such as flight paths over water while on an ASW mission. The upper panels above the flight displays control autopilot settings and radar inputs. Flanking the tactical display are two FMS (flight management system) panels. These enable the crew to adjust comms frequencies, plot waypoints, and read engine data. The central quadrant of levers controls auto throttles, speed brakes, stabilator trim, and engine thrust control levers or throttles. *Author*

This is the P-8A overhead console above both flight crew members. To the left of the console is the HUD and a white cabinet containing a HUD symbol projector. There are five rows of panels connected to navigation, electrical readouts, cockpit and exterior lighting, engine starting, pitot probe heat, fuel cross-feed, anti-icing, hydraulic pumps, the windshield washer and three-speed wipers, yaw dampers, and spoilers. *Author*

P-8A center pedestal between flight crew seats. At the very top are three red T-handles. Pulling these activates the fire suppression systems for the number 1 engine, APU, or engine number 2. Radios and communications selectors / volume controls flank weapons-bay-stores release, jettison, and arming of weapons. At the bottom center is the rudder trim setting. To right of this is the air-to-air refueling panel, with receptacle lights and stabilator trim override. At the lower left is the EW panel, with settings for options regarding the electronic-warfare suite. *Author*

A jump seat is shown here stowed, at the aft end of the cockpit. An observer, check pilot, or relief crew member can help out or else enjoy the view. *Author*

Aft of the right emergency exit is the galley. This view shows the stove and control panel for lights and to power up the appliances. The lavatory is an integral part of this section. *Author*

Above the right-forward emergency exit hatch is this space with an escape rope inside. The rope allows egress from the plane if a ladder or other way out is not available. *Author*

These two aircrew rest seats are immediately to the right as you enter the P-8A through the normal forward entry door. Turning left is the path to the cockpit. *Author*

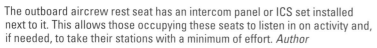

The outboard aircrew rest seat has an intercom panel or ICS set installed next to it. This allows those occupying these seats to listen in on activity and, if needed, to take their stations with a minimum of effort. *Author*

This view shows the entire galley arrangement in a P-8A. This unit is provided as a complete assembly by the vendor. The manufacturer installs it, connecting it to wires, pipes, and fuselage rails dedicated to it beforehand. *Author*

Past the galley/lavatory, on the right side, is this cabinet, which has several electronics racks for power distribution throughout the aircraft. An identical cabinet is on the left side. A large volume of cooling air is ducted into this section. *Author*

This multifunction panel allows the aircrew to access the power distribution hardware. Aircrews can access systems, monitor and adjust power flow to components, and isolate or interrogate system alarms. *Author*

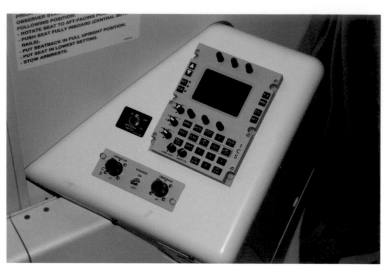

This is the port (*left*) side of the observer's station. The seat can move inboard or swivel. A padded elbow cushion below the window reduces fatigue. A sliding window shade is fully open at right. *Author*

The right observer's console has a window defog switch and intercom cord plug-in sockets for the station occupant and observer. The ICS intercom system panels link all crew members together. *Author*

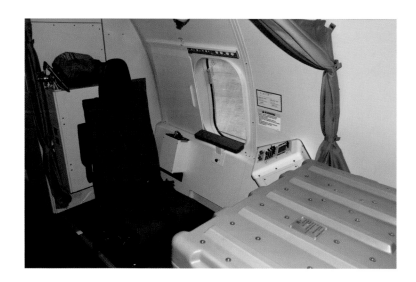

The starboard (*right*) seat is facing aft. It has a full set of restraint straps that release by turning an integrated harness knob. Pulling the black knob below the elbow cushion adjusts the height. *Author*

During a joint US/Ukrainian navy exercise in the Black Sea, Sea Breeze 2017, a Ticonderoga-class cruiser is seen from the right observer window of a P-8A of VP-16. *Justin Stumberg / US Navy*

Directly across from the five operator station consoles are these crew-ditching seats. They face aft, since this is the most effective, safest position in which to absorb deceleration forces if a P-8A had to land in the water. All seats have head restraints and integrated harnesses. These two closest seats are designated crew stations 16 and 17, with the label on the cabin wall showing the nearest exit and the actual location within the crew compartment. A large duct for the engine precooler and draw-through valve, protected by an aluminum guard, is at the lower right. *Author*

The first operator console station aft of the left-side observer area is the TACCO (tactical coordinator) position. The TACCO is the senior person who choreographs the entire mission operation underway. Tasks are delegated to the other operators as the TACCO supervises, while assessment and execution of actions occur with the objective of achieving a favorable outcome. Scenarios such as search and rescue (SAR), ELINT/SIGINT (electronic/signals intelligence), ASW, and ASuW all are team efforts. The TACCO can display and interact with many menus of mission-specific items as the flight proceeds, and can look at anything else the other crew members are working on. Laid over the lower display screen is a multi-image scene showing two plots of a "God's eye" view of the aircraft path, with the lower image showing the status of communications settings. *Author*

Next to the TACCO position is this station to the left as you move aft down the cabin, used by the Co-TACCO, or second tactical coordinator. The station has a pair of 24-inch displays, identical with all of these consoles. To the left of the keyboard is a joystick to interact with the MX-20 optical sensor. Above it is an emergency oxygen mask, rigged for quick donning in case cabin pressure drops. The lower screen has an overlay placed that shows a typical split-image display used for a tactical scene and weapons status. Four wing pylon stations are simulated to show AGM-84 Harpoon antiship missiles; the five weapons-bay pylons are toting Mk. 54 torpedoes. *Author*

The center station seen here, and the two farther aft, are used by enlisted aircrew. The TACCO can feed mission data to the three consoles on the basis of an individual's level of security clearance and experience in certain aspects of the mission, such as sonobuoy tactics, optical-sensor operations, or radar utilization. This station's lower screen overlay shows readings transmitted back to the P-8A from a bathythermograph device that provides data on salinity and thermal layers beneath the ocean surface. These variables are used to maximize information collection from other devices, such as active sonobuoys. *Author*

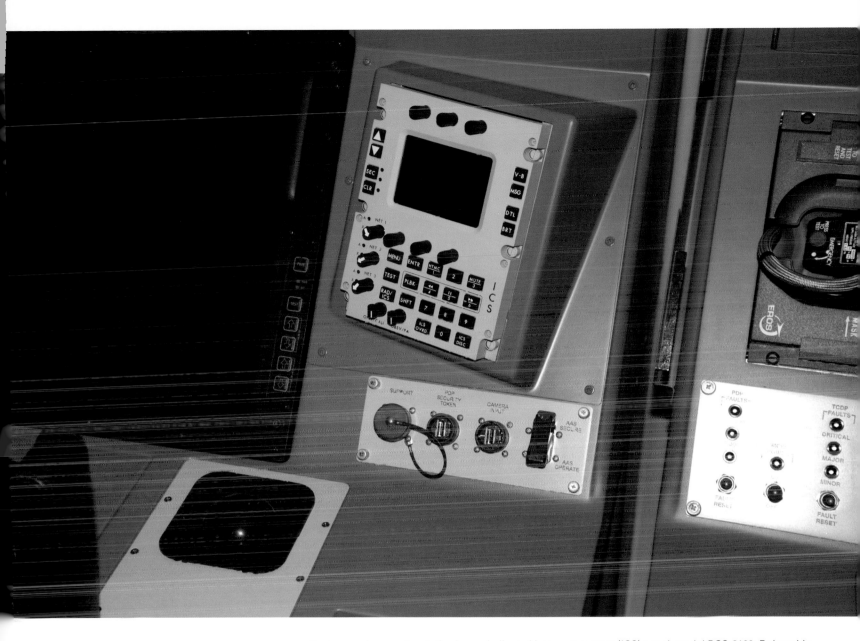

Each console operator station has a dedicated intercom system (ICS) panel, model DCS-2100. Below this is where an individual will insert a security token, which is read to determine the person's level of clearance to view and interact with mission hardware. As experience grows, so does access to more mission-related activities. A red guarded switch activates or turns off the AAS (acoustic assessment system). A trackball is used by the operator to work within various displays and to designate labels or buttons in assorted menus to control mission systems. All crew operators wear headsets to communicate clearly above the noise levels in the cabin as the plane flies. *Author*

This is the fourth MCW (monitoring and control workstation) position. It shows graphic overlays of an image (*at top*) obtained by the MX-20 optical sensor, located on the belly of the plane in a retractable compartment. The joystick seen previously can be used to zoom the optics in or out (from a wide-angle to a zoomed-in view), with the option of changing from normal vision to infrared-band scenes. All of what is seen can be recorded for later playback during flight or at a postflight debriefing. The bottom screen shows waterfall displays of undersea contacts provided by a deployed pattern of sonobuoys. A waterfall display shows the most recent data at the top of each of the twelve small screens. Over time, the new data is shown over the older signals, causing the images to move down. This can quickly show operators a history of any set time frame, from a few minutes to over thirty minutes, if desired. *Author*

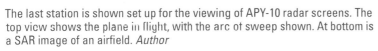

The last station is shown set up for the viewing of APY-10 radar screens. The top view shows the plane in flight, with the arc of sweep shown. At bottom is a SAR image of an airfield. *Author*

P-8As can accommodate a sixth MCW console. This one has been secured just aft of the left overwing escape hatch. The cabin was designed with the ability to adjust to mission demands. *Author*

At the forward end of the communications-racks cabinet are rows of panels with KY-100 and KGX-40A radios. Smoke detectors are present, with zeroized panels used to reset components to their factory settings. *Author*

This is the communications cabinet along the right side of the cabin. Across from this is the location for a sixth operator console, if it has been installed. Numerous grills allow air to flow in to keep the interior components cool. *Author*

Aft of the comms cabinet is this area for the aircrew planning table. Straps hold table leaves in place during taxi/takeoff and landing phases of flight. An ICS panel is placed above the center of the table, accessible to the four crewmen. Cabin ventilation vents are at the top of the photo and can be individually adjusted. The dark strip with red arrows on the floor lights up for ten minutes during a crew evacuation, showing personnel where to go to find the nearest exit *Author*

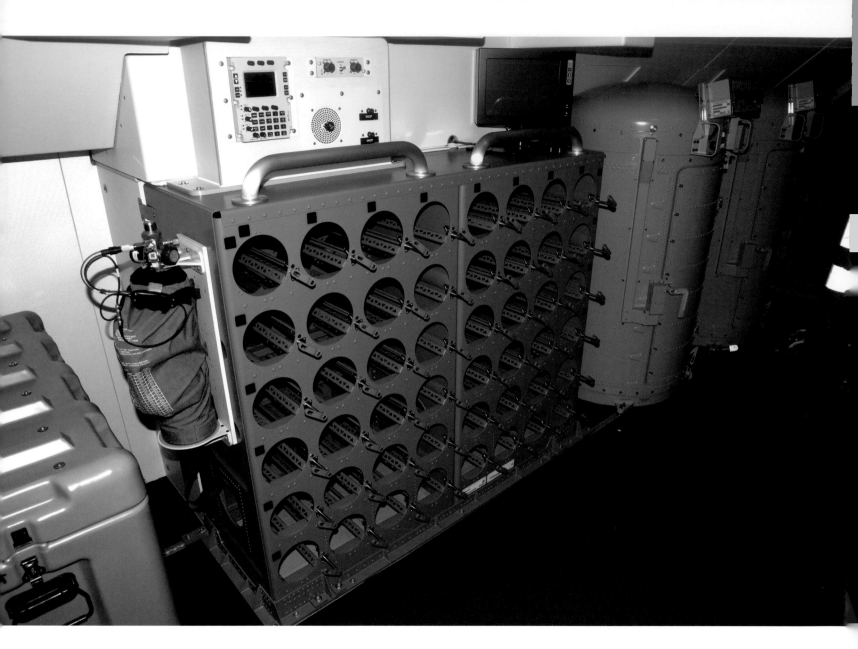

Past the planning table, along the right side, is this rack capable of holding forty-eight sonobuoys. Attached to the left wall is a portable oxygen cylinder. To the left of this is a partial view of a large cabin storage container. Sonobuoys are manually brought aboard and stored horizontally. As buoys are used, the rotary launchers can be reloaded in flight. The rows are labeled so that keeping track of different types of buoys is made easier. *Author*

Sonobuoys are loaded into racks by Aviation Ordnanceman 2nd Class Nick Casas of VP-47 during RIMPAC 2018, while this P-8A was at Pearl Harbor, Hawaii. *Kevin A. Flinn / US Navy*

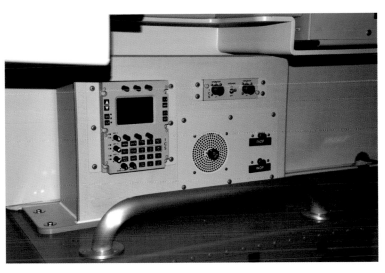

An ICS panel is placed above the right sonobuoy rack, so that while crew members work in this area, they can be connected to audio through their headsets and comm cords. *Author*

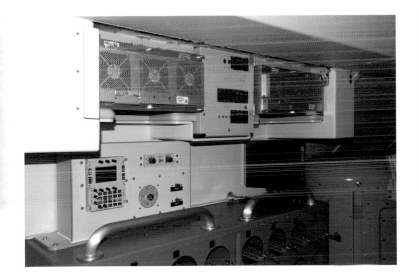

These fans above the right-side sonobuoy racks are used to cool satellite antenna equipment. Rows of push-pull circuit breakers are in the center of the pair of fan housings. *Author*

This left-hand rack is directly across from the other one. Aft of the rack is a partial view of one of the pressurized sonobuoy rotating-carousel launchers. *Author*

The P-8A can be outfitted with a pair of pressurized rotary carousel sonobuoy launchers on the right side. The door with a yellow handle opens so that the buoys can be loaded. Above the door is a manual pressure relief valve. *Author*

The left side has a single ten-round launcher, which can launch a buoy every three seconds. Up to forty can be deployed on a single air pressure charge of 5,000 psi. It can also fit buoys of various diameters. *Author*

This panel operates the ten-round launcher. The carousel can be rotated to a set number for loading. Before the door can be opened, the unit must be depressurized first. *Author*

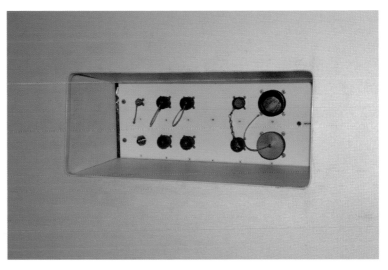

The upper surface of the cabin wall has these connections for data reception/transmission. Just outboard of this wall are sets of surface contact radiators to dissipate heat. *Author*

On this P-8A, one of the right-hand launchers has been taken out of the aircraft. The wiring harness seen here is reconnected when one is placed at this position. *Author*

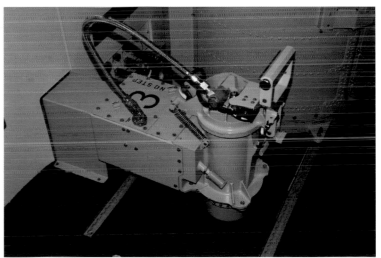

One of these single-sonobuoy launchers (SSLs) is mounted in the aft cabin floor. This one is on the left side, beside a rotary launcher. Opening the chute is done by lowering the yellow handle. *Author*

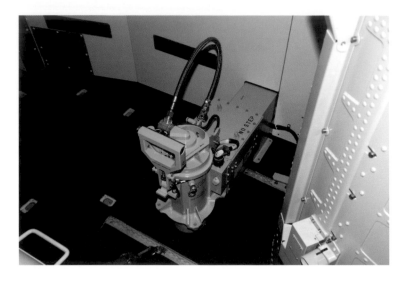

This elevated view shows the floor-mounted launcher secured over the launch tube and wall fitting; the unit weighs 37 pounds. It can drop the Mk. 39 EMATT simulated ASW target. *Author*

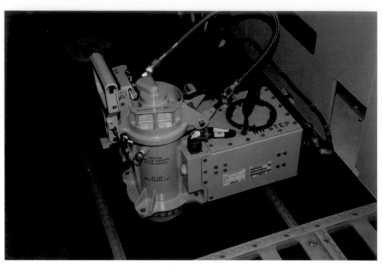

This one is located along the right side, aft of the rotary units. The handle seen on the gray box section is used to grip the end of a sonobuoy securely. *Author*

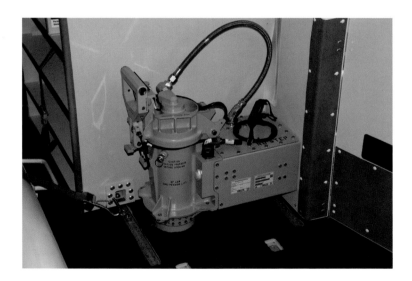

The second left-hand side SSL, located next to a cabinet used to store emergency gear. The small valve below with a ring is pulled manually to release any excess air pressure. *Author*

A Mk. 58 marine location marker (smoke flare) near the free-fall chute. It is also used to drop sound underwater signal (SUS) devices, or to jettison cabin gear. *Author*

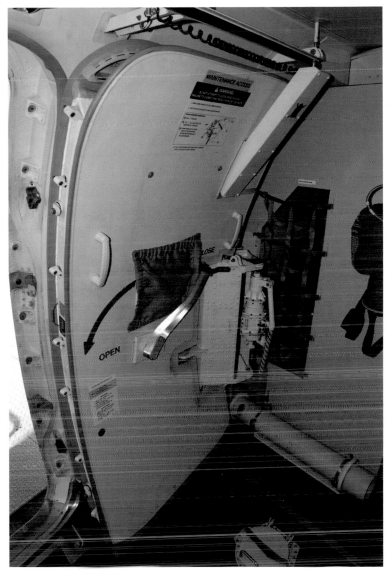

Naval Aircrewman (Operator) 2nd Class Clark Urbin is ready to drop a Mk. 58 smoke flare from the free-fall chute of a P-8A, during the search for the missing Malaysian Airlines plane MH370. *Keith DeVinney / US Navy*

The open right-aft maintenance door, with a partial view at the bottom of the free-fall chute. It has no pneumatic assist to push objects down the chute. It is used only at low altitudes at sea-level air pressure. *Author*

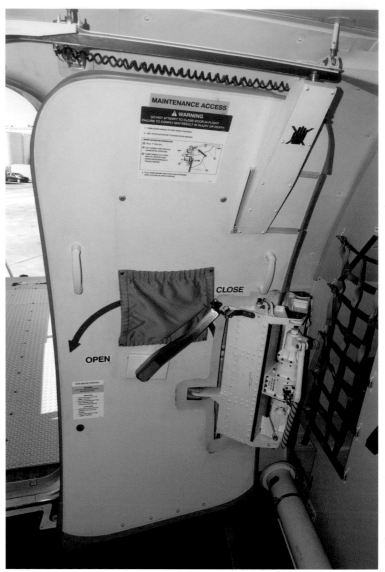

Aft of the left-hand-side SSLs is this locker for storing gear, such as these LPUs (life preserver units) used by the aircrew in the event of a water ditching. They automatically inflate upon contact with water. *Author*

The open P-8A left-aft maintenance / emergency exit door open. It is a plug-type design, fitting into the fuselage section when closed. After it is opened, it slides forward on rails above, to provide a clear entry point for personnel/equipment. *Author*

P-8A, BuNo 167951, article T1 / N541BA, being used to test the effects of aerodynamic buffeting on the opened weapons-bay doors. This test was conducted in March 2011, while the plane was assigned to NAS Patuxent River in Maryland. *Liz Goettee / US Navy*

P-8A Deployable Sensors, Weapons, and External Radar

Quickstrike mines: These are dumb or unguided bomb casings modified to be used as mines that are dropped over water or land. The process of adapting is the same as done for converting these into "smart" laser-guided munitions. A bomb has a kit attached, with a nose fuse and tail fins with or without a parachute, depending on the flight delivery profile chosen. Three types of Quickstrike mines are the Mk. 62, which is the Mk. 82 500-pound bomb version, the Mk. 63 1,000-pound mine (a modified Mk. 83), and the Mk. 64 2,000-pound bomb type. Two methods used to detonate such mines are by acoustic (activated by sound waves of an object generated by land vehicles or ships passing over them) or by seismic sources. These involve vibrations emitted as a truck convoy or seagoing vessel approaches. Mines are easy to lay down, and difficult for the defender to eradicate. This makes them very effective when used for area-denial operations in harbors or in terrain such as the approaches to a narrow mountain valley.

Sonobuoys: In 1941, the first ship-deployed sonobuoy was tested to detect German U-boats. It weighed 60 pounds and was not well suited for use in a marine environment. It evolved, during 1942, into a test of these upgraded buoys that detected the propeller noises of a submerged submarine, the radio signals being received by an overhead blimp. The first air-deployable sonobuoy weighed 15 pounds, encased in a cylinder about 3 feet in length, with a 5-inch diameter, later to be called the A-size-type buoy. The cylinder itself was a resin-coated thick paper tube. The ends were capped off with disks of wood. The bottom one had a water-soluble seal that allowed the buoy to sink after a time. All the materials that were used were ones that were not critical to the overall war effort. The first practical air-launched buoy, the AN/CRT-1, had a parachute and antenna. The radio transmitter in the hertz/kilohertz range (300 Hz to 8 kHz) had internal batteries and a hydrophone. A further developed model was known as the ERSB (expendable radio sonobuoy). The manufacture of thousands began, and in 1943, the improved AN/CRT-4 was tested, having a directional hydrophone that rotated three to five times each minute. The war ended before it was ever used in combat.

Tactics for using sonobuoys were developed. Aircraft would fly in cloverleaf patterns, dropping different-colored buoys, with each color corresponding to a different radio frequency. Usually the first one released by hand or from a bomb bay over a suspected contact was purple. Others would follow, such as red, orange, blue, and yellow ones. Buoys had dye markers so aircrews could maintain a visual record of where they were on the sea surface. At night, a low-intensity light was strapped to the buoy. If more battery power was necessary, extra cells were taped to the buoy cylinder.

In the mid-1950s the AN/SSQ-1 began development. It had a rotating hydrophone set at a depth of 50 feet and had a one-hour battery life. It became known as a B-size device, since it was 6.875 inches in diameter and 60 inches long. Also by this time, sections of the undersea SOSUS (sound surveillance system) network were in operation. Submarines passing over these sensors relayed data to ground stations. Air bases would dispatch aircraft that could consistently determine the locations of underwater craft by means of deployed patterns of sonobuoys.

Sonobuoys continued to improve during the Cold War era as submarines made advances in operating at increased depths and ran more quietly. Up to that time, buoys listened only passively for noises emitted from a target. The addition of active sound generation initially involved exploding a small depth charge near the buoy sensors, which reflected sound waves off a submarine hull. These would be detected by the buoy and relayed to the orbiting aircraft. The AN/SSQ-15 active buoy eliminated the need for carriage, handling, and deploying depth charges. It produced a continuous wave (CW) signal in the 26 to 38 kHz range. Further models included types such as the AN/SSQ-41, which replaced early passive types and employed the LOFAR (low-frequency analysis and recording) method. It streamed four hydrophones from 60 to 300 feet below the surface, and it could transmit data over thirty-one channels. The AN/SSQ-57 introduced a calibrated LOFAR array of expanded coverage from 10 to 20,000 Hz. Aircraft could also deploy these buoys at faster speeds and higher altitudes. With the SSQ-57, airspeeds of up to 380 knots were possible at heights up to 25,000 feet. DIFAR (directional frequency analysis and recording) passive buoys were fielded as the AN/SSQ-53 in the mid-1960s. Hydrophones were aimed in specific directions to listen for and pass along noises detected to the ASW aircrews.

The 1970s saw the arrival of AN/SSQ-77 vertical-line-array DIFAR or VLAD buoys, used to enhance submarine-related signals while filtering out other noises such as surface ships underway. The DIFAR hydrophone was located in the center of the array of omnidirectional hydrophones. A new A-size active buoy, the AN/SSQ-47, replaced the B-size SSQ-15, generating a pulsed signal every ten seconds between the 13 and 19 kHz bands. The AN/SSQ-50 CASS (command-activated sonobuoy system) replaced the SSQ-47, giving aircrews the means to emit signals or ping when they desired active mode to be engaged. A further

development of this mode was in the AN/SSQ-62 DICASS (directional command-activated sonobuoy system), in which a sonar transducer was lowered to various depths. CW waves could be sent in desired directions and results transmitted back to the aircraft over one of ninety-nine preselected radio data-link channels. This allows for many buoys to be used, each one transmitting on its own unique set frequency. The AN/SSQ-101 ADAR (advanced deployable acoustic receiver) became available in the 1990s. Upon landing in the ocean, five arms extend, spreading a forty-element sensor array that captures/relays data upon detecting sound waves from another active buoy.

Torpedoes: The P-8A carries the Mk. 54 MAKO lightweight hybrid torpedo. Up to five can be hung and released on racks inside the weapons bay. This version combines the warhead and propulsion sections of the Mk. 46 with the Mk. 54 homing hardware. It is suited for use in littoral regions as well as in blue-water combat. Its diameter is 12.75 inches (324 mm), its length is 106.9 inches (2.72 m), and it weighs 608 pounds (276 kg). Cost per round is estimated as $839,320 in FY 2014 US dollars. P-8A launch constraints are an airspeed of 340 KCAS (knots calculated air speed), flaps retracted, and 300 feet AGL (above ground level) or higher. Underwater speed is about 46 miles per hour (74.1 km per hour). The guidance system uses active/passive search, with active homing. The warhead is 96.8 pounds (43.9 kg) of PBXN-103 explosives, with an explosive yield equal to that of 238 pounds of trinitrotoluene (TNT). The Mk. 54 REXTORP (recoverable exercise torpedo) simulator can also be dropped, and it weighs approximately 406 pounds.

The P-8A will also carry the Mk. 54 high-altitude long-range-flying torpedo known as HAAWC (high-altitude antisubmarine warfare capability) add-on kit. This variant uses a standard Mk. 54 weapon and attaches deployable wings and tail fins for stability. The ALA (air-launched accessory) package also includes a GPS antenna, flight control computer, and battery power to operate flight control surfaces. With this capability, the P-8A does not have to fly at low altitudes, close to the target. In a shallow-water littoral tactical scenario, this also means the plane will not be vulnerable to shore-based antiaircraft defenses. A P-8A can launch this HAAWC-modified weapon at altitudes up to 30,000 feet, eliminating time spent descending to lower altitudes and speeds to engage a submarine or surface ship. If released at a 30,000-foot altitude, the torpedo would glide for about ten minutes. If another target is preferred over the original one, the new coordinates can be updated to change the flight path. It can also be updated with new targeting data by other friendly airborne platforms. At a set height above the water surface, the wings/fins are jettisoned, a stabilizing parachute deploys, and the torpedo assumes its normal operation once underwater. A contract of $23.2 million has been spent so far on HAAWC development.

AGM-84 Harpoon: These are usually carried (four AGM-84 / three AGM-84K SLAM-ER) on the underwing pylons. If the winged AGM-84K SLAM-ER (standoff land attack missile–extended response) is used, it is commanded in flight by the AWW-13 data-link pod, which the aircraft must carry on another pylon. The standard Harpoon uses GPS guidance and can be launched in the general direction of a target, turning on its radar seeker when in close range. If released with only target-bearing data, it can activate radar shortly after being fired. If the target is missed, it can fly around for a second attack pass. RAM (radar-absorbing material) is incorporated into the missile body to reduce detection by hostile radars and possibly be shot down. Allied nations such as Australia, Denmark, Greece, the Republic of Korea, Kuwait, Japan, the Netherlands, and Saudi Arabia are some countries that operate Harpoon in various subtypes, mainly aboard warships as the RGM-84.

APS-154 AAS: The P-8A has flown with an external radar installed, located under the forward belly section in a long, slender, canoe-type pod. Designated the APS-154 AAS (advanced airborne sensor), it provides capabilities similar to that of the single-side-looking APY-7 radar, used by the USAF E-8C JSTARS (Joint Surveillance Target Attack Radar System) platform. An earlier version of APS-154 has also been flown on a P-3C, being labeled as the APS-149 LSRS (littoral surveillance radar system). Both are used to enhance tactical awareness in the monitoring of and countering hostile actions while gathering intelligence, surveillance, and targeting data. The radar is a dual-sided AESA (active electronically scanned array) with MTI (moving-target indicator), SAR (synthetic aperture radar), and ISAR (inverse synthetic aperture radar) modes. These modes create photo-quality images of land or sea features and objects that can be used for tactical planning. When targets to be engaged are found, the P-8A can pass along this data to a weapon in flight or can stream the information to another platform such as a surface warship, another aircraft, or a ground station. The radar also has other uses, including jamming of signals and detecting low-flying objects such as cruise missiles or radar-evading aircraft, using terrain-masking (nap-of-the-Earth flight or NOE) techniques. The AESA array can also overwhelm hostile radars with radiated energy and generate false echoes of imaginary targets in a tactic known as spoofing.

UNI-PAC II Air drop survival kit: This versatile item can be filled with medical supplies, a self-inflating multiperson life raft, water, food, spare parts, or clothing. It can be tossed out of an opened side door or off an open cargo ramp or released from a weapons pylon in a munitions bay. In a tactical mission operation, it can be filled with weapons, ammunition, or communications gear to resupply special-operations teams on the ground. The P-8A can dispense these from the aft weapons bay at speeds of approximately 200 knots indicated airspeed (KIAS). A training shape that simulates the weight and size of the unit can also be used during exercise events to familiarize aircrews with handling and deployment.

At NAS Jacksonville in April 2014, a captive air-training missile, CATM-84D, is raised to a P-8A pylon by a VP-30 "Pro's Nest" aviation ordnance crew. *Jason Kofonow / US Navy*

This AGM-84D has a yellow band, indicating a live warhead. The brown band at the far end shows that a live rocket motor is installed as this Harpoon is loaded by a VP-30 team. *Juan S. Sua / US Navy*

An AWW-13 data-link pod is moved by Aviation Ordnancemen Bionica Riley and Ivan Sannicolas of VP-10. It is used on the P-8A to guide the AGM-84K SLAM-ER. *Shannon R. Smith / US Navy*

An inert AGM-84 Harpoon is dropped by a P-8A of the Royal Australian Air Force (RAAF) during RIMPAC 2018. View is from the right observer's window. *Nicci Freeman / RAAF*

A VP-4 "Skinny Dragons" aviation ordnance team poses by P-8A, BuNo 168757, after loading this AGM-84D Harpoon antiship missile to the inboard starboard underwing pylon. This is a completely live round, as seen by the yellow and brown bands. In this air-launched mode, the missile has a range of 120 nautical miles. Speed after launch is Mach 0.85, with 100 pounds of fuel supplied to an internal turbojet with 600 pounds of forward thrust. The warhead weighs in at 488.5 pounds of semi-armor-piercing HE (high explosive). The weight of the air-launched version is 1,145 pounds. It has been used in combat in the Gulf of Sidra, in the Persian Gulf, and in Operation Desert Storm. *Juan S. Sua / US Navy*

P-8A, BuNo 168434, has an inert ATM-84 Harpoon on show during an open house at NAS JAX in October 2014. The fins are not attached during the loading/unload procedures. *Author*

Air-training missile (ATM)-84 hung on the right outboard pylon. The nose radome is fragile, so when transported and handled, a protective cover is always installed. *Author*

This view of the ATM-84 is looking outboard from the wing root area. A yellow plug seals the aft-section exhaust outlet. It is used by many allies as the ship-launched variant. *Author*

A right-side nose quarter-angle view of P-8A, BuNo 168434, shows the Harpoon as well as a Mk. 54 torpedo, being displayed to the public at NAS Jacksonville in 2014. *Author*

Aviation Structural Mechanic 2nd Class Daniel Carrilho moves a pair of SSQ-53F DIFAR (directional frequency analysis and recording) sonobuoys in LAU-126 launch containers. *Sean Spratt / US Navy*

SSQ-53B sonobuoy minus launch container. At the top is the parachute and antenna, with sea anchor and hydrophones at the bottom. In the center are electronics and batteries. *Author*

Seaman Joseph Skramstead, Seaman Jasmine Jackson, and Petty Officer 3rd Class Marcus Batemon load racks and check sonobuoys in a P-8A while at Rota, Spain, before a patrol flight. *Keith Estes / US Navy*

Checking channel settings is Naval Aircrewman (Operator) 1st Class Jason Lankhorst of VP-45. The P-8A in this case is participating in the Northern Coasts event in 2016. *Keith DeVinney / US Navy*

Sonobuoys transmit data on preset channels. This can be set as well as operating depth and modes on these SSQ-101 sonobuoys stacked on pallets. *Author*

A sonobuoy contained in the tan LAU-126 canister is handled by Naval Aircrewman 2nd Class Karl Shinn of VP-16. He will then turn a lever to hold it in place. *Keith DeVinney / US Navy*

SSQ-101 sonobuoys are stored vertically, eventually to be loaded aboard a P-8A for use in operational missions. The SSQ-101 versions are of the A size, and of the ADAR (air-deployed active receiver) type. Once the buoys are launched out of these containers, hit the water, and activate (taking up to 240 seconds from water entry), they lower a pentagonal-shaped array of forty hydrophones. Sound waves are then generated. Any signals received are beamed up to the aircraft to be displayed and analyzed further. Each weighs 31 pounds (14.1 kg), operates on internal batteries from 4.5 to 6 hours, and has a shelf life of five years. Operating depth can be set for 65 feet (19.8 m), 300 feet (91.4 m), or 500 feet (152.4 m). *Author*

A nose fuse is attached to a Mk. 62 Quickstrike mine by Mineman Petty Officer 1st Class Daniel Gregware. This mine was used during the BALTOPS 2018 exercise. *Emily Copeland / USAF*

A bomb jammer moves a completed Mk. 62 mine. The colors show this to be an inert training device, which also is easier to find once the recovery phase begins. *Emily Copeland / USAF*

Mineman Petty Officer 3rd Class Zachary Bourassa attaches the tail kit. The location is at RAF Fairford in the United Kingdom, during the Baltic Sea multinational drill. *Emily Copeland / USAF*

A Quickstrike mine loaded onto a P-3C wing pylon. The fins spread open after release, creating aerodynamic drag to slow the mine down before it enters the water. *Jakoeb Vandahlen / US Navy*

A Mk. 54 lightweight torpedo displayed next to a P-8A at the NAS JAX airshow. This is a REXTORP (recoverable exercise torpedo drill version). *Author*

The REXTORP is lighter in weight than a warshot and has the white nose and fluorescent tape applied for easy visual sighting in order to be picked up and used again. *Author*

Once dropped free of the weapons bay, this protective container splits open and falls away, allowing the stabilizing chute to unfurl and steady the torpedo in the air. *Author*

On an actual torpedo, the nose section contains an active sonar. Behind the sonar is the guidance section, warhead, and propulsion unit, including steering fins and propellers. *Author*

The P-8A has performed in many search-and-rescue calls for assistance. A UNI-PAC II survival kit is dropped, containing a life raft to fishermen adrift at sea. *US Navy*

P-8As are often intercepted by Chinese J-11 fighters as they conduct freedom of navigation flights. "Blue 24" is seen in close formation near disputed Pacific Islands. *US Navy*

Fishermen adrift for eight days were found and aided by a P-8A of VP-8. They called a patrolling vessel to the scene so that they could be saved. *US Navy*

This detail image taken by the MX-20 sensor shows the missile armament load-out on the J-11. Such photos can provide intelligence on fighter capabilities. *US Navy*

Despite adding a weapons bay, underwing hardpoints, and fairings on the fuselage sides, the P-8A retains most of its original planform, as shown by this pair of Poseidons assigned to VP-4, the "Skinny Dragons," as they fly in formation over the East China Sea while forward deployed to conduct antisubmarine warfare and freedom-of-navigation flights. *Juan S. Sua / US Navy*

The "Golden Swordsmen" of VP-47 gathered in Skywarrior Theater at NAS Whidbey Island, Washington, to celebrate the operational milestone of 1,000 flight hours logged with the P-8A in March 2018. *Kevin A. Flinn / US Navy*

A P-8A shivers while on the ramp at Keflavik, Iceland, while on a deployment for ASW training in the North Atlantic in April 2017. *Matthew Skoglund / US Navy*

A P-8A is towed into a hangar at Whidbey Island by Aviation Machinist's Mate 3rd Class Brandon Marchant. Others watch the wingtips for adequate clearance. *Juan S. Sua / US Navy*

Aviation Technician Airman Blake Robbins deices a P-8A of VP-4 before a flight out of NAS Whidbey Island in February 2018. *Juan S. Sua / US Navy*

P-8A, BuNo 169340, is in a routine maintenance check at NAS JAX. Hydraulic lifts make access to upper sections of the planes much easier. *Author*

On jacks during an A-10 check, performed every 2.5 years, is this VP-4 P-8A during a free-fall test of the landing gear. In order to conduct such inspections, the entire plane must be raised up off the hangar floor. Black power cords are connected into the external power receptacle. The nose landing gear falls into the slipstream as it lowers, the airflow aiding in pushing it into place before landing. *Juan S. Sua / US Navy*

The flight line at NAS JAX is full of P-8A Poseidon aircraft, the P-3C becoming an ever more rare sight in 2018. Included in this picture are BuNos 168428, 168763, 168854, 169011, and 169337. On-base facilities did not have to be modified or enlarged to accommodate the conversion from one type to another. *Author*

The forward entry door on P-8A, BuNo 169340, has had the inside panels removed in the course of a maintenance check. The many holes allow for inspection access. *Author*

This angle shows the double-slotted arrangement. Flaps provide slower approach speeds and greater control when in takeoff and landing phases of flight. *Author*

In this view, the flap actuators and tracks are exposed with the aerodynamic fairings angled down. The flap style used is of the double-slotted-type Fowler design. *Author*

Should an engine fire occur, this storage cylinder under high pressure will expel the halon agent into the engine. This is located in the pylon above the exhaust nozzle. *Author*

To mark the occasion of the arrival of the first P-8A to NAS Jacksonville for VP-30 "Pro's Nest" in March 2012 are, *from left to right*, VAdm. Allen G. Myers, commander of Naval Air Forces; Adm. Mark Ferguson, vice chief of naval operations; Undersecretary of the Navy Robert O. Work; Alvin Brown, the mayor of the City of Jacksonville; and RAdm. Michael W. Hewitt, commander of patrol and reconnaissance groups. The aircraft is BuNo 168428, manufacturer's serial number (MSN) 40808. *Christopher Servello / US Navy*

Kadena, Okinawa, November 2018. The Japanese Self-Defense Forces (JSDF) chief of staff, Adm. Katsutoshi Kawano, and the aircrew of a JMSDF (Japan Maritime Self-Defense Force) P-3C Orion pose with Adm. Phil Davidson, commander of the US Indo-Pacific Command and the flight crew members of a P-8A Poseidon. Both nations were participating in a joint operations series of exercises. Such maneuvers are done on a routine basis to allow aircrews to work together in a variety of mission scenarios, from antisubmarine hunting to search-and-rescue and antiship warfare tactics. *Kevin A. Flinn / US Navy*

While visiting Misawa, Japan, in March 2016, Lt. j.g. Lance LaFlanne of VP-16 conducts a tour of the P-8A cabin to an interested group of Japanese dignitaries. Such tours at locations around the world show the current capabilities of the P-8A type, promoting dialogue and enhancing relationships with allies while showing foreign nations the hardware, the skills of the aircrews, and the realities of US policies regarding the security of sea lines of communication and the rights to freedom of navigation on the high seas and in the airspaces above them. *Samuel Weldin / US Navy*

During a visit of a unit to the Republic of Korea navy (RoKN) to Kadena, Okinawa, in November 2018, RAdm. Ki Jae Kim, commander of RoKN Air Wing 6, and Capt. Brian Erickson, commander of Task Force 72 (TF-72), strike a pose with their groups in front of a P-8A. The aircraft is part of a deployment to the Pacific region to operate in surveillance, security, and intelligence-gathering missions.
Kevin A. Flinn / US Navy

A pair of P-8A Poseidon aircraft make a pass over a packed Everbank Field in the city of Jacksonville, during a pregame ceremony as the National Football League's Jacksonville Jaguars hosted the Indianapolis Colts in December 2015. Military units regularly participate in such events, usually timed to coincide with the singing of the National Anthem, with a huge American flag unfurled and held above the midfield. Both NAS Jacksonville (JAX) and NAS Mayport are located in the Jacksonville area.
Timothy Schumaker / US Navy

SSgt. Duane Mitchell of the 374th Maintenance Squadron Transient Alert signals a P-8A to give it parking commands at Yokota Air Base, Japan. *Donald Hudson / USAF*

A P-8A takes on a load of jet fuel. Total capacity is 10,856 US gallons (71,040 pounds). Tanks are in the wings, with three main tanks in the fuselage. *Shannon R. Haney / US Navy*

Aviation Structural Mechanic 3rd Class Rowdy Murphy has taxi wands crossed, the universal hand signal to stop as a P-8A ends a mission at Ault Field. *Juan S. Sua / US Navy*

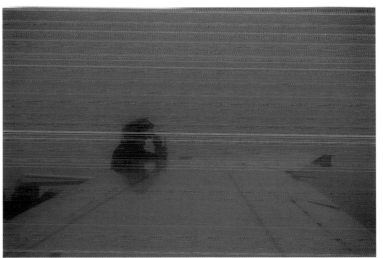

Even in inclement weather such as thick fog, the work must go on, as Aviation Structural Mechanic 2nd Class Marie Deleon of VP-4 is busy on the starboard wing. *Juan S. Sua / US Navy*

Much of life in the Navy is devoted to public relations and humanitarian assistance. These two activities are big factors in maintaining strong relationships with American allies and promoting the armed forces as instruments of good in areas hit by floods, earthquakes, tsunamis, and mudslides. Much time and effort in a Navy career can indeed be spent in the performance of these gestures of aid in the course of many deployments. In a moment of camaraderie and friendship with members of the Japan Self-Defense Forces, Naval Aircrewman 3rd Class Lucas Dahms of VP-10 gives a smile and thumbs-up pose during a P-8A tour for the group. *Samuel Weldin / US Navy*

A P-8A of VP-8 flies over DDG-92 *Momsen*, a US Navy Arleigh Burke–class guided-missile destroyer. These two platforms have the ability to operate independently, or together. The aircraft can patrol up to hundreds of miles ahead of the ships of a surface action group. The P-8A can monitor, track, and, if necessary, eliminate surface ships or submarines, long before they can threaten friendly combatants. The destroyer can attack land targets with Tomahawk cruise missiles, such as a surface-to-air missile (SAM) site, which can pose a danger to the P-8A if it is operating in littoral regions. Both can share information in real time by means of data links such as the CDL or Link-16 JTIDS networks. *Daniel Rodriguez / US Navy*

P-8As, BuNos 168853 and 168758, at rest on the ramp at Joint Base Hickam, Hawaii, in the run-up to another RIMPAC exercise. Once the aircrews board and activate systems, check operating status, and taxi to the active runway, they will depart to the air for flights involving simulated detection, tracking and hunting of submarines, surface warships, mining, and gathering intelligence. They could also quickly convert to search-and-rescue mode if a request for help is broadcast. The P-8A is a popular and effective platform, in use by American and allied nations to secure sea lanes, probe the ocean depths for hostile vessels, and make it known that in a tactical scenario, potential adversaries should take heed of Poseidon and of the Trident it carries, in the form of torpedoes, mines, missiles, and bombs. To those lost or stranded at sea, the sight of a P-8A is one of relief at being discovered, aided, and saved from an undesirable fate. The P-8A, with its highly motivated, enthusiastic, and proficient aircrews, maintainers, and supporting infrastructure, is set to become the prime aerial asset, taking the place of a tried, tested, and well-proven P-3 Orion. *Kevin A. Flinn / US Navy*

Acronyms/Initialisms

AAS	acoustic assessment system; advanced airborne sensor	**CASS**	command-activated sonobuoy system
ADAR	advanced deployable acoustic receiver	**CDL**	common data link
ADS-B	automatic dependent surveillance–broadcast	**CMDS**	countermeasures dispensing system
AESA	active electronically scanned array	**CRT**	cathode ray tube
AEW+C	airborne early warning + control	**CW**	continuous wave
AGL	above ground level	**DAB**	defense acquisition board
AGM	antiship guided missile	**DDG**	destroyer-guided missile armed
AIP	antisurface warfare improvement program	**DF**	direction finding
ALA	air-launched accessory	**DICASS**	directional command-activated sonobuoy system
AoA	angle of attack	**DIRCM**	directional infrared countermeasures
APU	auxiliary power unit	**EAB**	emergency air breathing
ASuW	antisurface warfare	**EATS**	extended-area test system
ASW	antisubmarine warfare	**ECS**	environmental-control system
ATC	air traffic control	**EEC**	electronic engine control
ATM	air-training missile	**EGT**	exhaust gas temperature
BAC	Boeing Aircraft Corporation	**ELINT**	electronic intelligence
BALTOPS	Baltic operations	**ELT**	emergency locator transmitter
BRU	bomb release unit	**EMATT**	expendable mobile ASW training target
BuNo	Bureau Number	**EMDS**	electromechanical-expulsion deicing system
C3	command control communications	**ERSB**	expendable radio sonobuoy

ESM	electronic support measures		**JSDF**	Japan Self-Defense Force
EW	electronic warfare		**JSTARS**	Joint Surveillance Target Attack Radar System
FADEC	fuel and digital engine control		**JTIDS**	Joint Tactical Information Distribution System
FMS	flight management system		**KCAS**	knots calculated air speed
FOV	field of view		**KIAS**	knots indicated air speed
FS	federal standard		**kVA**	kilovolt-ampere
FSD	full-scale development		**LAIRCM**	large-aircraft infrared countermeasures
FY	fiscal year		**LAPS**	liquid air palletized system
GAS	GPS antijam system		**LED**	light-emitting diode
GPS	global positioning system		**LOFAR**	low-frequency analysis and recording
HE	high explosive		**LPU**	life preserver unit
HUD	head-up display		**LRAACA**	long-range air ASW-capable aircraft
ICS	intercom system		**LRIP**	low-rate initial production
IDG	integrated drive generator		**LRMPA**	land-based maritime patrol aircraft
IFF	identification friend or foe		**LRRA**	low-range radio altimeter
INMARSAT	international maritime satellite		**LSRS**	Littoral Surveillance Radar System
ISAR	inverse synthetic aperture radar		**MAD**	magnetic-anomaly detector
ISR	intelligence, surveillance, reconnaissance		**MCW**	monitoring and control workstation
ISR&T	intelligence, surveillance, reconnaissance & targeting		**MIDS**	Multifunctional Information Distribution System
JMSDF	Japan Maritime Self-Defense Force		**MILSTAR**	military strategic and tactical relay

MLG	main landing gear	**SAM**	surface-to-air missile
MMA	mission maritime aircraft	**SAR**	search and rescue
Modex	also known as "buzz number"	**SDD**	system development and demonstration
MSN	manufacturer's serial number	**SIGINT**	signals intelligence
MTOW	maximum takeoff weight	**SINKEX**	sinking exercise
MUOS	multiple-use objective system	**SLAM-ER**	standoff land attack missile–extended response
MWS	missile-warning system	**SOSUS**	sound surveillance system
NACA	National Advisory Committee for Aeronautics	**SPS**	sonobuoy positioning system
NiCad	nickel-cadmium	**SSL**	single-sonobuoy launcher
NLG	nose landing gear	**SUS**	sound underwater signal
NOAA	National Oceanic and Atmospheric Administration	**TACCO**	tactical coordinator
OBIGGS	onboard inert gas–generating system	**TCAS**	traffic alert and collision avoidance system
PAXSIL	Patuxent River Systems Integrated Laboratory	**TCDP**	tactical communications data network
PBXN	polymer-bonded explosive	**TNT**	trinitrotoluene
PCHRD	pilot color high-resolution display	**TPS**	tactical paint scheme
PMAWS	passive missile approach warning system	**UARSSI**	universal aerial refueling receptacle slipway installation
psi	pounds per square inch	**UAV**	unmanned aerial vehicle
RAM	radar-absorbent material	**UHF**	ultrahigh frequency
RFP	request for proposal	**UV/IR**	ultraviolet/infrared
RMPA	replacement maritime patrol aircraft	**VHF**	very high frequency
RoKN	Republic of Korea Navy	**VLAD**	vertical-line-array DIFAR
rpm	revolutions per minute	**WTAI**	wing thermal anti-icing system
RWR	radar-warning receiver		